HIDDEN HISTORY

of

NANTUCKET

Frank Morral & Barbara Ann White

MARK WHITE, PHOTO EDITOR

THE
History
PRESS

Published by The History Press
Charleston, SC 29403
www.historypress.net

Copyright © 2015 by Frank Morral and Barbara Ann White
All rights reserved

First published 2015

Manufactured in the United States

ISBN 978.1.62619.705.3

Library of Congress Control Number: 2015934855

Contents

Acknowledgements

This book has been a labor of love, and we have been supported by several people along the way. First and foremost, Mark White, our photo editor, worked hard to gather photos from which we could choose, many of which he shot himself. Then, he worked hard to ensure that their quality was ready for publication. Fundamental to that process was the incomparable team at the Nantucket Historical Association's Research Library. Maria Henke, the photograph archives specialist, worked tirelessly alongside Mark, helping him to search the extensive archives for the best possible photos. She then scanned them to the highest possible quality. Elizabeth Oldham, research associate, and Betsy Tyler, the Obed Macy Research Chair, were ever helpful in pointing our research in the right direction.

Thanks also to Toby Morral and Linda Morral for their support throughout and to Frances Karttunen for her expertise on Nantucket's African American community.

We also have to acknowledge the assistance of The History Press, in particular Tabitha Dulla, who shepherded us through the process and was available to answer our many questions along the way.

I

Greasy Luck

Methoughts I saw a thousand fearful wrecks;
Ten thousand men that fishes gnaw'd upon;
Wedges of gold, great anchors, heaps of pearl,
Inestimable stones, unvalu'd jewels,
All scatter'd in the bottom of the sea.
—*William Shakespeare,* King Richard III

S hortly before his brother drowns him in a butt of sweet Malmsey wine, George, the Duke of Clarence, recounts his nightmare of drowning in a sea full of riches. No place on earth knew better the perils and wonders to be found in the sea than the island of Nantucket in its great days of whaling. Its riches lay not in gold or heaps of pearls but in the greasy luck to be found in hauling in the whales that made the candles and lamp oil that lit the nation in the eighteenth and nineteenth centuries.

But the luck ran out. Whale oil was displaced, and with it, the island's prosperity shrank and the population dwindled from its high of nearly 10,000 in the 1840s to 2,797 in 1920. Just when it seemed greasy luck would never return to the island, a miracle happened in the sudden appearance of over four hundred tons of coconut oil moving across the waters and onto the beaches of Nantucket in early April 1921.

After a fifteen-thousand-mile journey from the coconut lands of Southeast Asia, the British cargo steamer *Gaelic Prince* stopped briefly in Boston to unload part of its cargo of fruit, sugar and coconuts. From Boston it was headed to Brooklyn and its soap factories with nine hundred tons of coconut oil in its hold. But it ran into trouble at four o'clock on Wednesday morning, March 30, 1921.

A little off course, the *Gaelic Prince* ran aground on a "knuckle" or protrusion of the Great Round Shoal about eight miles east-northeast of Nantucket. Despite seven days of urgent effort by a fleet of tugs and lighters, and assistance from the coast guard cutter *Acushnet*, the *Gaelic Prince* could not be budged from where it lay stuck on the shoal.

When it came to saving the ship or the cargo, the choice was easy. Nine hundred tons of coconut oil heated to a liquid consistency sufficient to be pumped out of the ship's hold was dumped into the cold April waters of the Atlantic, supposedly never to be seen again.

Wits on the mainland suggested so much oil would calm the restless waters of the Atlantic and be a boon to keeping mermaids well soaped and clean. One described it as the "milky whey."

Coconut oil congeals at temperatures below seventy degrees Fahrenheit and melts at higher temperatures. When the *Gaelic Prince*'s cargo hit the cold waters of the Atlantic, the coconut oil became blobs, cakes and slaps of white stuff of all sizes from smaller than a pie to as large as a steamer trunk. Although no one realized it at first, "greasy luck" had returned to Nantucket.

The oil was pumped out of the *Gaelic Prince* on Wednesday, April 6, freeing the ship from the shoal. By daylight the next day, white stuff had drifted toward the island from the east. The "ocean resembled curdled milk," and the beaches soon looked "ice rimmed." Enterprising islanders took to their boats to gather it up. As east winds blew it on shore, first on the beaches of Wauwinet and Quidnet and then, days later, more broadly across the island—to the Jetties, Brant Point, Children's Beach, Polpis and Madaket—islanders brought their baskets, buckets, bags, wheelbarrows, baby carriages, horse-drawn carts, trucks and cars to the greasy work of bringing in the coconut oil harvest.

Almost at once, enterprising housewives of the island bought up all the lye and oil of lavender and sassafras in the local pharmacies and began making soap. Never had so much soap been made on the island or soap so fitting for the island, since among its properties was the ability to work up a good soapy lather even in the salt water of the sea. It was said that in the golden days of whaling, whalers would carry coconut soap for when freshwater bathing was not to be had.

Eddie Backus in the Nantucket Historical Association's oral history collection tells how his mother made the soap: "You had to first put it on the stove in a pot of water, the cakes, & let it melt. And then set it aside and let it congeal again—because there was so much salt water & seaweed & bits & pieces in it…[then] strain it out and get the oil pure back again. And then she proceeded to make soap."

Fine homemade soap was all well and good. But in the knowledge that this unexpected harvest had traveled fifteen thousand miles on its trip to the island, those who drew the white stuff to themselves by bucket load, fishing boat and truck knew in their hearts there must be money to be found in the greasy stuff somewhere, a belief confirmed on April 9 when John Killen, agent for the Board of Marine Underwriters, placed a large notice in the *Inquirer and Mirror* ordering, "All parties having, or finding, any of the cargo from the steamer *Gaelic Prince* to deliver the same to him." The coast guard cutter *Acushnet* had also been ordered to remain in the Nantucket harbor until the following Tuesday, which seemed ominous. Was the government looking to collect duty on all this oil?

Rumors were rife. Some believed soap factories in New Bedford and elsewhere would pay five cents a pound for the white stuff. Word from

USCGC *Acushnet* operated from Woods Hole, with cruising grounds of Buzzards Bay, the Nantucket Shoals and adjacent waters. *Naval History and Heritage Command.*

Lloyd's of London suggested that the cargo had been valued at $400,000, the equivalent today of about $5,500,000, but only once it reached the New York area's soap factories. The urgent questions now became what was it worth in Nantucket and to whom did it belong?

Never, it seemed, was there a better chance of getting something for nothing, even though most did not consider hauling in tons of greasy stuff from beaches and the ocean exactly "nothing."

Time, however, was of the essence. All present knew by now that their harvest was at the mercy of the weather. A warm spell would transform the cakes of congealed oil into a liquid that all too quickly would melt into the streets, byways and beaches of the island and then flow back into the sea.

E.H. Hicks in his poem "Beautiful Ile of the Sea," published in the *New Bedford Mercury* and reprinted by the *Inquirer and Mirror*, tells the story up to the point where turning the oil to money and identifying who owned it required deciding:

> *"Pour oil upon the troubled wave,*
> *And let the ship go free,"*
> *So spake the stranded* Gaelic Prince;
> *And oily was the lee.*
> *Those tons of oleaginous*
> *Ex-freight solidified:*
> *And then they drifted down upon*
> *Nantucket, far and wide.*
> *The canny island folk were dumb*
> *At sight of whitened shore.*
> *But soon, recovered from amaze,*
> *They scooped it up galore.*
> *For "While there's oil, there's soap," said they,*
> *And shipped it to the main,*
> *And then went back unto the beach*
> *And scooped some in again.*
> *"Nan-tucket!" then the owners cried,*
> *And called up the police,*
> *So now the salvage question looms,*
> *Of who shall have the grease.*

According to the *Inquirer and Mirror*, the island's paper of record, not since the sewer controversy thirty-seven years before or the arguments over allowing automobiles on the island had there been so much interest in a town meeting as there was for the coconut oil harvest and what was to be done with it.

At the initial meeting on Friday, April 15, full delegations were on hand from Wauwinet, Polpis, Quidnet, Madaket, 'Sconset and elsewhere on the island. It was standing room only in the town hall, and many could not squeeze in at all.

The main question at hand: who could be trusted? From the beginning, it was clear that no trust could be put in anyone representing a shipping line or insurance company. According to George Harral, who later would become a key player, an insurance man "told the Islanders if they sold any of the oil they would be arrested. The natives laughed long and loud at this threat, as their jail would only hold two."

Although it was suggested repeatedly that negotiations be put in the hands of a committee, the suggestion did not meet with favor. Everyone present wanted to be involved.

The claim by Mr. Koehler, representing the Prince Steamship Company, that the islanders did not own the oil and only had a half interest as "salvors" also did not meet with favor. Nor did his saying the steamship's agents would sell it for two cents a pound on the mainland. When the meeting asked how much he would pay for it on the island, the answer was "nothing." Only after it was transported and purchased would a half interest come back to the island.

John Garland said he would rather leave his oil in his barn and "let it melt" than take "a paltry two cents a pound." Albert L. Coffin suggested hiring a lawyer. James H. Wood countered that "the further away the meeting kept from a lawyer the better off it would be."

Again the suggestion to form a committee was ignored. Everyone had a stake in the action; everyone wanted to be involved. All that could be decided was to meet the next day, Saturday, when an oil buyer would be present.

The news was not good. At the next meeting, the price seemed to have fallen to one cent a pound. On hearing this, the overflow group laughed, and more threatened to let the oil melt back into the sea.

When a formal motion for a committee was introduced, only sixteen of the three or four hundred attending the meeting even voted. Ten were in favor, six against. But that was enough for the motion to pass and a committee to be formed. On Wednesday, April 20, the committee report was delivered to a meeting as large as the previous two had been.

The key to the solution was George S. Harral, a summer resident and the owner of the Harral Soap Company in New York. Harral told his story in a

Ship *Nantisco* unloading barrels. *Nantucket Historical Association.*

May 1949 *Inquirer and Mirror* column. His involvement, he wrote, had begun with James A. Backus of Wauwinet, "one of the true-blue of the Island," calling him at his home and asking him to come to the island and help with the coconut oil problem.

Harral himself offered four and a half cents a pound after the oil had been refined. Of the $27.50 per ton after expenses, Nantucket would receive half, or $13.75 per ton. It was the best offer yet. Nantucket agreed to put it in Harral's hands.

Harral began by arranging for the three-masted coal carrier *Nantisco* to ship the oil. Since coal dust would do little to enhance the oil, barrels and bags in great quantity were required to protect the precious oil from the insides of the *Nantisco*. Five thousand bags were brought from Providence alone, and thousands of other bags and barrels were located on the island.

For three days, the oil arrived at the dock from every corner of the island to be weighed, credited to the owner, bagged, barreled and crammed into the ship's hold. According to Harral, it was during this period that "Captain" Backus said, "There were many arguments and hard words and it was no place for a Methodist minister."

Arguments or not, on Sunday, the sign went up: "Vessel full, No more oil accepted." Islanders had brought 386 loads to the scales, and 337 tons were stored in the good ship *Nantisco*. So much oil still remained that the two-master *A.M. Jagger* was contracted to take the extra 70 tons still looking for passage to the New York area, which left many tons, it was thought, still on the island for those not tired of making their own soap.

When the vessels arrived at City Island in New York and were boarded by customs officers, it was realized there was no duty owed since the oil had not been shipped from a foreign country but from Nantucket, the only time such a cargo had ever been known to ship from within the United States to another port in the United States.

A buyer was found in New Jersey, and the *Nantisco* and *A.M. Jagger* were towed to the Jersey Meadows. According to Harral, "Large kettles and boilers were brought to the docks and the next day, as

Coconut oil made from oil pumped out of the *Gaelic Prince*. *Nantucket Historical Association.*

the coconut oil was unloaded it was thrown into these kettles, melted and put into drums and sold to the soap-makers."

With all expenses deducted and profits divided, the oil netted the Nantucketers for their work "six-tenths of a cent a pound, or $12 a ton."

So that is how "greasy luck" came again to Nantucket. One can only wonder how much this manna from the sea may be responsible for altering the future fortunes of the island. Before the coconut oil bonanza, the island had been on a long decline. Rock bottom was the population of 2,790 in 1920, the lowest in all the time since the first census count of 4,555 in 1790.

After the coconut oil harvest of April 1921, the wind seemed at the island's back. By 1930, population was up 31.5 percent to 3,678. All it took was another seventy years for it to reach 9,520 in 2000, breaking 1840's record high when, thanks to the whaling industry's greasy luck, the count was 9,012.

2

One Island, Two Nantuckets: One Black, One White

W hen most people think about racial segregation, they think about the South during the years of Jim Crow laws. Less understood is the segregation of the North, even during the heyday of abolition before the Civil War.

Nantucket's black community mostly lived in the area then called New Guinea that extended from Orange Street to Pleasant Street, an area known

View looking south from the Unitarian tower on Orange Street. In the distance and along the perimeter of town are fringes of the New Guinea neighborhood. *Nantucket Historical Association.*

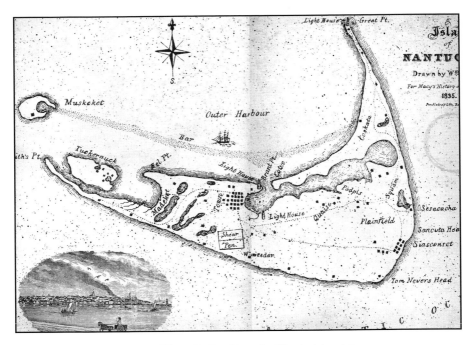

1835 map of Nantucket by William Coffin. *Nantucket Historical Association.*

as Five Corners. Among the few descriptions of New Guinea is a mid-1830s advertisement for a building lot in the neighborhood. It was advertised as a "delightful spot composed of persons of correct habits, living by their own industry, and in perfect harmony."

Although few records have survived, there is evidence of a small black community on the island as early as 1710. Most were brought involuntarily as slaves. William Gayer's will in 1710 left a room in his home and half of a "leanto" for life to "Africa, a Negro once my servant." Unlike the more fortunate Africa, most slaves on the island did not receive inheritances from their owners, instead appearing in wills as transferable property. In 1718, Stephen Hussey left "a Negro woman named Sarah" to his wife and sons. He also left "a negro boy named Mark" to one of his sons and a "negro girl Dorothy" to his daughter.

A free black community on the island began to grow as some slaves were manumitted. In 1716, a monthly meeting of the Society of Friends, or Quakers, recorded that it "is not agreeable to Truth for Friends to purchase slaves." It was the first Quaker monthly meeting in the world to make such a declaration. Nantucketer Elihu Coleman's tract against slavery in 1729 was the second such essay written by an American, and it went through several national editions. This did not mean, however, that everyone on the island heeded the call to emancipate slaves, and slaves continued to be held and appear in estate lists. In 1735, for example, Jonathan Pinkham's estate included a man named Sambo, and in 1740, Samuel Baker's included unnamed slaves. Thomas Brock's inheritance in 1750 included an unnamed "Negro woman." Benjamin Coffin possibly manumitted the last three slaves on Nantucket in 1775, just one year before the American Revolution.

The free black community was augmented by fugitive slaves and by black people attracted to work on whale ships, some from the United States and others from elsewhere as whaling ships picked up workers along the way. In 1790, there were 76 people of color living in their own households in New Guinea. By 1820, Nantucket had about 275 nonwhite residents out of a population of just over 7,000. By 1840, at the peak of whaling, the nonwhite population had grown to 576 out of a total population of around 10,000. Included in these numbers were those who were left from the original population of Wampanoag, many of whom intermarried into the black community. By the 1850 census, one of seven people of color was classified as mixed race or "mulatto."

The records do not support the notion that Nantucket was a major stop on the Underground Railroad, but it is clear that fugitive slaves worked on Nantucket whalers, and some chose to settle on the island. It is easy to understand why fugitives would be attracted to the island where work was available, society was somewhat tolerant and there was an established black community.

Nantucket was not entirely segregated. Black people were employed throughout town as domestic workers, and they worked in the industries peripheral to whaling, including as coopers, block makers, blacksmiths and rope makers in integrated workshops. Barbershops owned by black men catered to an integrated clientele, with several shops in the heart of town.

The black community created separate institutions within its neighborhoods. This was partly a matter of convenience and partly in a spirit of entrepreneurship but also a response to segregation by mainstream Nantucket. The records are inconclusive as to whether the white churches on the island were segregated during this time. An unsigned letter to the editor in 1841 hinted that they were by asking, "Do you not in your *Christian* churches recognize a negro seat or pew?" Certainly social organizations and clubs did not admit black members. This extended to separate temperance societies and even, for a short time, a separate abolitionist organization, although by 1839, the local Anti-Slavery Society was integrated. For a time, even the Atheneum, a private museum and library, barred black people from borrowing books. In response, white abolitionist Obed Barney opened a lending library over his store on Main Street, open to everyone.

The steamship that ran from the island to New Bedford restricted blacks from the first-class section on the upper deck. In the mid-1830s, E.F. Mundrucu filed a complaint with the steamship company because of its mistreatment of his family. Mundrucu claimed he had paid for first-class tickets, but they were not allowed to sit in the first-class section. When the family refused to move to second class, the captain had them taken off the boat.

There were grocery stores, a bakery and boardinghouses owned and operated by black families for their neighbors. John Pompey operated a dance hall for several years in the 1820s by the windmill on Upper York Street. The two black whaling captains on the island, Absalom Boston and Edward J. Pompey, both owned stores after they retired from the sea. Boston also owned a boardinghouse for black sailors. William Whippey and his wife, Maria Ross, opened the Kanaka Boarding House for the Pacific Islanders who found themselves on the island between whaling voyages. The sign for their boardinghouse now is housed in the Nantucket Whaling Museum.

Eventually, two black churches were erected in New Guinea. The first written record of "a colored church" appears in 1821, when the newspaper reported that black Nantucketers had a "room fitted up for that purpose," as well as "a preacher of their own." The African Meeting House, located at the corner of York and Pleasant Streets, was probably built in 1824. A variety of names were used to refer to the church until the last congregation disbanded in 1888. It was called the African Church, the York Street Colored Baptist Church, the Colored Baptist Church and the Pleasant Street Baptist Church. It was affectionately nicknamed "the Little Church Around the Corner" in its final decade. The meetinghouse was a multipurpose building, serving as a church and a school. Lectures on abolition and temperance were held there as well as concerts. It was a place to have picnics and community festivities, and it was where smallpox vaccinations were administered. Now owned by Boston's African American Museum, the African Meeting House is open for tours.

The other black church was Zion Methodist Episcopal (AMEZ) Church, commonly referred to as Zion's Church. It was organized in 1832. Long since gone, it was located on Upper York Street. In 1838, an anonymous white man, probably abolitionist Nathaniel Barney, wrote a letter to the newspaper describing what he saw that year on the Fourth of July at the Zion Church, which was nothing fewer than 150 well-dressed black citizens paying "the

African Meeting House on the corner of York and Pleasant Streets, built around 1825 by and for the black community of New Guinea. *Nantucket Historical Association.*

The Historic Coloured Cemetery located behind Nantucket Cottage Hospital on Mill Hill. *Mark White.*

strictest attention" to an antislavery speaker. He noted that there was "no peace, no liberty for the colored man in these Independent States," so no cause to celebrate Independence Day. In opposing slavery, they appeared "to feel they were about *holy* work."

Segregation also applied to the graveyard. Behind Nantucket Cottage Hospital is the cemetery originally set aside for Nantucket's people of color. The graves of generations of black Nantucketers can be found there. Tours of the cemetery can be arranged through the African Meeting House, and a catalogue of those buried there is on the Nantucket Historical Association's website.

The most dramatic example of segregation on Nantucket, however, revolved around education. In 1826, the black community created a school for its children at the African Meeting House, known as the African School. The school opened its doors to about forty students a full year before the town created public schools, proof of the value the black community put on education. The school was absorbed by the public school system the next year.

Anna Gardner, the secretary of the Nantucket Anti-Slavery Society, taught at the school for four years, and it was during her tenure that a controversy about integration arose. Gardner had strong abolitionist credentials. When she was only six years old, her family had successfully hidden Arthur Cooper and his family from bounty hunters at their home on Vestal Street, saving them from being seized and taken back into slavery. In addition, Absalom Boston was a family friend and had introduced Gardner to William Lloyd Garrison's abolitionist newspaper, the *Liberator.*

When Nantucket established its first public high school in 1839, admission was based on passing an entrance examination. Eunice Ross, the fifteen-year-old daughter of African-born James Ross, passed the exam but was denied admission to the high school because of her color. The battle that resulted over her denial dominated island politics for the next seven years, dividing

Anna Gardner (1816–1901) wearing the locket given to her by her students at the African School. *Nantucket Historical Association.*

neighbors and families. In a special town meeting in June 1839, Edward M. Gardner, a cousin of Anna's, proposed to "permit coloured children to enter all or any public schools." This was the opening salvo in the battle over school integration.

To protest the segregation policy, trustees of the African Meeting House refused to allow the town to continue using their building. Rather than integrate, the school committee built another school down the street designated solely for the town's black children. Anna Gardner resigned in protest, refusing to teach in a segregated one-room schoolhouse while white children had the option of attending graded schools.

The black community met at Zion Church in 1842 to protest school segregation. They wrote an address to the "Inhabitants of the Town" asserting their right to have "their youth educated in the same schools which are common to the more favored members of this community." The town turned a deaf ear and continued to segregate schoolchildren.

In 1843, enough abolitionists were elected to the school committee to vote for school integration, even though the previous town meeting had voted to continue segregation. The school committee sent fifteen black children to the two previously all-white grammar schools and assigned white children to the school on York Street, thereby integrating it as well. Eunice Ross did not choose to attend the high school, presumably because, then in her twenties, she would have been so much older than her classmates.

The next year, however, the experiment with school integration was abruptly and brutally halted when the abolitionists were voted off the school committee and replaced with hardline segregationists. Within days, the committee ordered the re-segregation of the schools. The students at the grammar schools were publicly expelled in front of their classmates and ordered back to the re-segregated school on York Street.

To protest the expulsion, black parents pulled their children from the segregated school, an early example of a civil rights boycott. In the absence of black children, the school committee was forced to assign white children to the school in order to keep it open.

Having had no success through the local government, the integration leaders took their battle to the state legislature in Boston. Captain Edward J. Pompey and 104 other members of the black community submitted a petition in January 1845 describing the "insults and outrages upon their rights" on the island. Two petitions from white Nantucketers supported their claims. The anti-integrationists submitted two opposing petitions, arguing that the town had provided the black children with "an excellent school."

Eunice Ross, however, submitted the most compelling petition of all. In a firm and legible hand, she described how she had qualified to enter the high school but had been refused "on account of her colour."

State lawmakers agreed with Ross and her fellow petitioners. In 1845, they passed the first law in the United States to guarantee equal education to all students and gave their guardians the right to sue their towns for damages for noncompliance.

The battle seemed won, but it quickly became apparent that the island's establishment had no intention of complying with the new law. The school committee refused to integrate the schools, stubbornly insisting that the York Street school was equal to the other town schools, an argument echoed decades later in the Supreme Court's infamous *Plessy v. Ferguson* "separate but equal" decision.

Captain Boston prepared to sue the town on behalf of his daughter, seventeen-year-old Phebe Ann, who had been forcibly ejected from a grammar school. The school boycott continued into a second year but weakened as parents began to send their children back to the school on York Street so as not to deny them an education.

Once again, however, the political climate changed, and abolitionists were elected to the next school committee in 1846. Perhaps islanders were tired

Schoolchildren, black and white together, on West Dover Street in the old New Guinea neighborhood, circa 1880. *Nantucket Historical Association.*

of the issue and sensed that the lawsuit would go against them. Perhaps they were convinced by events off island as the country's abolition activity intensified, and the country lurched inexorably toward the Civil War.

Regardless of the reason, the school committee once again voted to integrate the schools. This time there was no backlash, and Captain Boston dropped his lawsuit.

While the controversy had been painful, the island is now justifiably proud of its role in the passage of the first legislation in the United States to guarantee equal education.

3

Cyrus Peirce Goes to Washington

Cyrus Peirce (1790–1860), first principal of Nantucket High School and director of the first normal school in the nation. *Nantucket Historical Association.*

C yrus Peirce enjoyed the mystery he generated on his train ride to Washington, D.C., in 1843, refusing to divulge the contents of the unwieldy cylindrical box he was carrying, leaving his fellow passengers to guess at what it held. The box was as big as a washtub, and he guarded it carefully, leading some passengers to speculate that Peirce was en route to the patent office to register a wonderful new invention. Peirce kept his silence.

The contents of the box were more precious to Peirce than any invention would have been. He was not a materialist; he was a man of principle who regarded his mission to the nation's capital as holy work. He knew that the battle in which he was about to engage was one that he had no hope of winning. The important thing was to fight injustice. Peirce's aim was to alter the Constitution and

George Latimer (1819–1896), fugitive slave. *Massachusetts Historical Society.*

dismantle the stranglehold of power that the South had in the House of Representatives in order to abolish slavery. Inside his box was a petition that aimed to do just that. He knew it was doomed and did not even know if he would have the chance to present it. He was undeterred.

George Latimer and his pregnant wife, Rebecca, were fugitive slaves who had fled from Virginia to Massachusetts. George Latimer was arrested in Boston in October 1842, when, by a stroke of very bad luck, a friend of their former owner recognized him. The fate of the Latimers became a cause célèbre in Massachusetts. Free Latimer Societies sprang up throughout the state, determined to prevent the couple from being returned to slavery under the Fugitive Slave Laws of 1793.

On Nantucket, the Free Latimer Society was co-chaired by Cyrus Peirce and Nathaniel Barney, both members of the Nantucket chapter of the Anti-Slavery Society. In his mid-fifties, Peirce was a well-known educator and reformer. Originally from Waltham, he had come to the island to teach after his graduation from Harvard. His marriage to Harriet Coffin connected him to one of the island's founding families. A passionate believer in the importance of public education, Peirce had been instrumental in convincing Nantucket voters to comply with the state law that required every town to have a free public high school, a law the town had flouted for decades. In 1839, Peirce had been chosen by the school committee to be the first principal of Nantucket High School.

After just one year as principal, Peirce left the island when he was offered the opportunity to create and direct the first publicly funded teacher training school in the United States. In 1837, Massachusetts became the first state in the nation to establish a board of education, and Horace Mann was appointed as the first secretary of education. Mann had become acquainted with Peirce on trips to the island in his new role and had been impressed by

Lexington Normal School, the first public teacher training school in the nation, 1839–1843. *Framingham State University Archives.*

his observations of Peirce in the classroom. Both men shared the belief that American democracy could not survive without an educated populace; both were passionate crusaders for public education.

Cyrus Peirce single-handedly wrote and taught the curriculum at the successful Lexington Normal School. In 1840, twenty-five young women graduates became the first professionally trained schoolteachers at public expense in the United States. (They were called "normal schools" from *écoles normales*, the name for teacher training schools in France.) Based on Peirce's success, two more normal schools opened in Massachusetts, one in Barre and one in Bridgewater. Neighboring states, including Rhode Island, Connecticut and New York, opened their own normal schools based on Peirce's curriculum, and within decades, normal schools had proliferated across the country, all based on Peirce's model.

But the work of running the normal school took a toll on Peirce's health, and he returned to the island just as the Latimer case was intensifying. At a three-hour rally held by the Nantucket Free Latimer Society, Peirce criticized American churches for their silence on the abolition of slavery, saying that in his fifty years as a churchgoer, he had *never once* heard a sermon preached against slavery.

THE LATIMER

AND

GREAT MASSACHUSETTS PETITION.

To the Senate and House of Representatives of the State of Massachusetts:

The undersigned citizens of the State of Massachusetts, earnestly desiring to free this commonwealth and themselves from all connection with domestic slavery and to secure the citizens of this state from the danger of enslavement, respectfully pray your honorable body,

1. To forbid all persons holding office under any law of this state from in any way officially or under color of office, aiding or abetting the arrest or detention of any person claimed as a fugitive from slavery.

2. To forbid the use of our jails or public property of any description whatever within the Commonwealth, in the detention of any alleged fugitive from slavery.

3. To propose such amendments to the Constitution of the United States as shall forever separate the people of Massachusetts from all connection with slavery.

NAMES.

The Latimer and Great Massachusetts Petition that resulted in the Personal Liberty Act of 1842, which forbade state officials from aiding in arrest, detention or delivery of a fugitive slave. *Massachusetts Historical Society.*

Eventually, both Latimers obtained their freedom from money raised across New England to purchase them from their owner. To prevent such future cases, Massachusetts passed the Personal Liberty Act that forbade judges, justices of the peace and other state officers from aiding in the arrest, detention or delivery of a person designated as a fugitive slave. The law also prevented slave owners from being compensated for their "property."

Despite the change in the law in Massachusetts, abolitionists knew that the Personal Liberty Act, while a step in the right direction, was insufficient because it would protect only the fugitives who made their way to Massachusetts and did nothing to help the approximately three million people enslaved in the country.

A petition drive, therefore, was launched in Massachusetts to amend the federal Constitution. It proposed basing representation on the number of *free* persons in a state; if passed, it would eliminate the unfair advantage the South had in the House of Representatives, where slaves were counted as three-fifths of a person in apportioning representatives.

The leader of Nantucket's petition drive was Peirce. Fresh from his success at the normal school, it is no surprise that he was given the honor of delivering the petition to Washington on behalf of the entire state.

Peirce arrived in Washington, D.C., on a cold day in mid-February, the streets slick with ice. On February 15, 1843, he spent the evening with John

Quincy Adams, the former president who was then serving in the House of Representatives. The two men strategized about how to submit the petition because the "gag rule" prohibited the submission of all petitions pertaining to slavery and abolition. It had been passed in 1836 and had effectively thwarted all discussion of slavery for years. Adams advised Peirce to meet with the other representatives from Massachusetts and assured Peirce that he would also meet with each of them.

The abolitionists in Massachusetts had gathered the signatures on narrow strips of paper. The petition had been pieced together and wound on a cylinder before Peirce left Boston. In Washington, Peirce had a revolving frame fitted to the cylinder that allowed the petition to unwind. It was Peirce's intention to unroll the lengthy petition in the House of Representatives to dramatically indicate what 51,680 names looked like. He wrote to a friend that the petition stretched "almost half a mile" and resembled a "new-fashioned barrel churn."

A week after Peirce's arrival, Adams attempted to present the Latimer petition; it was George Washington's birthday. Adams noted in his diary that the stormy day started with a military parade in Washington's honor. After the parade, the former president requested the House to suspend its rules to enable him to present a variety of petitions, "among which was the Great Massachusetts Latimer Petition." Adams wrote, "My Latimer petition so entirely covered my table that it left me no space for writing." John Brockway of Connecticut lent his friend his desk for the day.

Peirce described the scene more colorfully. He wrote that the huge petition sitting on Adams's desk angered the representatives of the slave states. "How the sight of that big roll did make those Philistines of the South rage and foam and stamp and gnash their teeth!" He said that they "looked daggers" at him for having been so bold as to deliver it. He wrote that they "cursed those who had signed it," wishing that they could be taken to a plantation and enslaved "to taste there the sweets of slavery."

Unfortunately, the southern majority succeeded in blocking Adams and Peirce. The motion to suspend the rules was rejected by a vote of 88–103. The huge petition suffered the fate of all the attempts to discuss slavery during the years of the gag rule.

After the session adjourned, Adams went to the clerk's office with a list of a variety of petitions with directions as to which committee they should be sent. He instructed the Latimer petition be referred to the Judiciary Committee. Furthermore, he demanded it to be "entered on the Journal of the House" to give it legitimacy.

A fragment of the Latimer petition to the U.S. House of Representatives, found by Barbara and Mark White in an undocumented file in the National Archives. *Mark White.*

Adams, however, did not succeed in the clerk's office either, and two days later, the petition was returned to him. It survives today in some unfiled and unorganized document fragments in a series of boxes in the Library of Congress, where my husband and I were lucky enough to find several pieces of it, including one with Peirce's signature. Unfortunately, the contraption Peirce built for it is long gone.

Despite his inability to submit the Latimer petition, Peirce did not believe the efforts of the Massachusetts abolitionists had been in vain. He had not expected to succeed. The abolitionists were well aware that the House of Representatives would not accept a petition negating the three-fifths compromise and altering the stranglehold the slaveholding states had in the House.

In a letter to the Nantucket *Inquirer,* Peirce wrote that the dramatic effect of taking the giant petition to the floor of the House had warranted the effort. He was pleased with the disruption it had caused and the publicity it had garnered for the cause. "I doubt not, in the least, it has effected vastly more for the great cause of human freedom, which we have at heart, by a hundredfold." He was proud of the part he had played. "For one humble individual of the goodly company of 50,000, and more, I am entirely satisfied with the good that has been done."

Peirce's optimism was misplaced, and he did not live to see the abolition of slavery or the bloody Civil War.

4

The Nantucket Civil War Monument

The Nantucket Civil War Monument is a graceful obelisk that stands alone in a little, awkward-to-use roundabout at the intersection of Main, Gardner and Milk Streets, an area called Monument Square. Even drivers familiar with the intersection wonder whether to treat the little circle as a rotary or ignore it and take the shortest way to their next street.

For islanders, the monument is part of the background of life on the island, something easily taken for granted, except perhaps on Memorial Day. Many know it relates to the Civil War but are uncertain if it memorializes all Nantucket's soldiers and sailors who fought in the war or only those who died in it.

Tourists often show more curiosity about the monument than islanders. After walking from town up Main Street past the historic houses built in the island's prosperous whaling days, they stop at the monument and really look at it. If nothing else, they absorb a sense that they stand in the presence of something profound in Nantucket history.

Much can be learned from a careful look at the monument. But much is also hidden. Beyond some familiar Nantucket names—Starbuck, Coffin, Chase, Folger—few know anything of those whose names are chiseled on its granite panels.

It was common in both the North and South after the Civil War to memorialize those who had fallen. Plans for tributes began before the war ended, and many were in place shortly after 1865. The monument in Quincy, Massachusetts, with its thirty-four-foot height and 105 names, was in place

Civil War Monument, 2015. *Mark White.*

by 1868. But Quincy, like most towns and cities in the North, prospered during the war. Nantucket did not. From the 1840s to the 1930s, the island lost population. It also suffered grievously in the war. Nantucket earned the name "the Banner Town of the Commonwealth" because so many of its men joined the army and navy. If, as is often assumed, four hundred Nantucket men served and seventy-four died between 1861 and 1865, nearly one of every five in service perished in the war. But the losses were actually heavier. Many died in the years after 1865 from war-related diseases and wounds.

Civil War monuments took many forms. A common one was the obelisk, a form passed on from ancient Egypt and Rome. The traditional obelisk is tall and four-sided, and its shaft tapers as it rises to a miniature pyramid at its peak.

The Nantucket monument at fourteen feet is a gracefully proportioned smaller version of the form. It stands in a circular plot of land where four streets converge, within an octagon of eight granite posts connected by rods low enough to step over. For some decades during the twentieth century, wire fencing kept viewers at a distance. The wire barrier is no more, and the monument stands as it did when first erected, although its surroundings have changed. At one time, the Town Building, home to the town court, stood on the corner of Milk and Main Streets, along with candle and whaling workshops and other commercial buildings. In 1874, when the monument was erected, some commercial buildings still inhabited the neighborhood, including a grocery store, but the town itself had moved toward the harbor.

The monument rests on a two-stepped pedestal, one or both of its stones supplied from the Round Top Mill on New Lane Street, taken down a year earlier. Above in dark polished stone are four panels, one to a side. The first, approached from lower Main Street, holds a dedication and a bas-relief of an anchor with a cannon resting in one of its flukes, a symbol in the eighteenth and nineteenth centuries of deceased sailors. Some feet above in bas-relief on the shaft itself are three stacked rifles decorated with a wreath, symbolic of soldiers who are no longer in the fight.

Three panels list in rough order of their deaths the names of seventy-four soldiers and sailors. The attempt to list soldiers and sailors in order of when they died breaks down most notably with the insertion of four late additions—Henry S. Folger, Charles R. Gruber, Peter C. Brook(s) and John Swain. They are placed at the bottom of the three panels without reference to date of death.

The lettering of "Erected 1874" chiseled into the two steps of the monument's base seems out of scale. By far the most visible, most readable, most prominent words on the monument, they perhaps express, with emphasis, the relief of finally doing justice to those who died in the war.

The monument's dedication reads:

ETERNAL HONOR
TO THE SONS OF NANTUCKET
WHO GAVE THEIR LIVES TO PRESERVE
A UNITED COUNTRY

Inherent in the dedication is a puzzle: which sons of Nantucket should be honored? What of those born on the island but living elsewhere when they enlisted? As Nantucket's economy faltered at mid-century, many departed the island to find work elsewhere.

Nantucket reached its nineteenth-century population peak in the 1840s with close to ten thousand people living on the island. It was the generation born at the island's high point of prosperity who largely fought and died in the Civil War.

The population drop after 1840 was precipitous. In 1860, island population was down more than a third to 6,094. Work was simply not available to

Dedication and date on the monument, as seen from lower Main Street. *Frank Morral.*

sustain a larger population. In fact, there wasn't enough work on Nantucket to sustain 6,094. Within ten years, island population had dropped to 4,123. Between the fire of 1846—which devastated the commercial area of the town, destroying the ports and much of the industrial base of the whaling industry—and the coming of the railroad to the mainland, making New Bedford a better distribution center than Nantucket for whale oil and whale-related products, the economy of Nantucket collapsed.

In a November 5, 1865 essay in the *Inquirer and Mirror* titled "The Past," the writer reflected on the glories of Nantucket's earlier years and the melancholy reality of its diminished present. He recalls "halcyon days, when our fleet of eighty sail whitened the Pacific, and our teams groaned with the weight of huge casks of oil—rich returns of long voyages in quest of the monsters of the deep." These glorious days are contrasted with the present, when "waning fortune was the destiny of all who continued in business." The writer looks at Nantucket's present and sees a double loss—of families divided and lives disrupted by the exodus of the young (and those not so young) looking for work elsewhere, as well as by those lost in war, killed in battle or by the diseases epidemic during the war.

Both groups are reflected in the writer's final lament:

> *Socially, what change! Sad memory brings the list of other days around us. What a loss is before us in memory of those, whose beauty, grace and vivacity made the numerous social gatherings of those other days delightful. We will not name them. The survivors need no aid in recalling the names of the loved and lost, or fallen into the sere and yellow leaf.*

The May 16, 1874 *Inquirer and Mirror* addressed the issue of what to do with those born on the island but who moved away:

> *A question as to non-residents, or men who, although natives of Nantucket, had removed, gained a residence elsewhere, and then enlisted, has given some trouble to the Committee; but it is evident that the names of such ought not, justly, to be counted here, as they are liable to be included in another list at the place where they enlisted.*

In fact, at least ten of the seventy-four on the monument enlisted to the credit of towns other than Nantucket. Whether a soldier or sailor is on the monument or not seems to depend on whether the *Inquirer and Mirror* published notice of his death and cited military service.

James Nichols Jr. did not receive such a listing and is not on the monument. He was born on the island and closely enough connected with it for the Barney Genealogical Record to record that he was killed in the war at Salem Heights, Virginia, on May 2, 1863. His photo is one of the few

James C. Nichols, sergeant, Company B, Rhode Island Second Infantry, one of those not on the monument. *Nantucket Historical Association.*

in the Nantucket Historical Association's collection of Civil War soldiers. Someone thought him sufficiently of the island to donate it.

At the time Nichols enlisted, he was a twenty-three-year-old machinist and a resident of Providence, Rhode Island. He was a full first sergeant in Company B, Rhode Island Second Infantry Regiment, when he was killed at Salem Heights, Virginia.

PLANNING THE MONUMENT

As early as December 27, 1862, following the deaths of eight Nantucket men at Fredericksburg, the committee laying out lots in the island cemetery for soldiers began thinking of ways to memorialize them. An intent was expressed to "open a subscription book" for funds to erect a monument "which will ever keep in remembrances the names of those brave men who fell in fighting our country's battles." But nothing more was heard of this plan.

In a sense, the first memorial was not a monument but an article in the *Inquirer and Mirror* on September 6, 1865, listing "our citizens who have died for Freedom." Sixty-seven names appeared in it listed by year of death, many with a few words about where, when and how they died. Most included the name of their regiment or the ship or hospital in which they died. Of the seventy-four soldiers and sailors on the monument, sixty-five were first listed here.

Titled "In Memoriam," the column is itself a memorial, even as it refers to "memorial halls" that Yale and Harvard plan to construct to honor their graduates "who have fallen on the battlefield." No physical memorial is suggested for Nantucket. Simply listing the names of the dead in the paper seems itself a memorial.

At the time the Nantucket monument was dedicated, credit was given Reverend Dr. F.C. Ewer as first to give public voice to erecting a Nantucket monument. Ewer was born on Nantucket in 1826 of a ship-owning family and educated in the Nantucket High School and Harvard College, class of 1848. Ewer's appeal for a monument was made in August 1866 at the "Second Annual Nantucket High School Alumni Festival." Nantucket, he argued, owed it to its "gallant dead" to "raise a monument that shall stand in her public square and bear down their names to a grateful posterity."

Dr. Ewer was one of those who left Nantucket. At this time he lived in New York, where he was pastor of Christ Church. Probably no occasion offered more fertile ground for proposing a Civil War monument than one addressed to alumni of the island's high school. Many in the audience would have attended school with those who died in the war.

The community picked up Ewer's suggestion two years later. On June 13, 1868, a special meeting was called to plan a suitable monument in memory of "those sons of Nantucket, who fell during the late Rebellion." The proposal was no sooner made than the town refused to vote money for a monument, not because it wasn't deserved, but because the town's debt was "already greater than we can bear." What bore the town down was clear: "We see our young men going abroad to find the means of living in other places, leaving a large proportion of unproductive persons at home, old men and females; while the business of the place is very slowly if at all increasing."

If the town could not fund the monument, hopes were that private donations, subscriptions and ticketed events could. Although the resulting monument might not be as elaborate as others might do, or the island might want, it would honor "the departed" and "grace our public square." Imagined was "a commemorative shaft," not something hidden away in a suburban graveyard or suggestive of the grave, but of "the battle and the sacrifice."

Our "public square" was proposed as the "only fitting place." Today it is unclear where this public square would have been at the time. Perhaps it was unclear then as well. No decision where to put the monument was made until it was already shipped from Churchill and Hitchcock in Quincy and on the island.

Dr. Ewer again served centrally in plans for raising money. He volunteered to lecture at the Atheneum, with price of tickets low enough for all to come, and proceeds to go toward the monument. The talk given was "The Antiquity of Man on Earth." Ewer argued that new facts had demolished the "'six thousand literal year' theory" of man's time on earth, a progressive speech for the time. Unfortunately, no record survives of the money it brought in.

In addition to lectures, money was to be raised by private subscriptions from residents and nonresidents of Nantucket, by fairs put on "by our women and tableaux given by our elder children." It was hoped that all would be involved. Throughout the money-raising effort, much depended on the "energetic ladies" of the island and the "nonresidents," those raised on Nantucket who had left the island to find their fortunes elsewhere.

Although funds were raised over the next five years, little more about the monument found its way into the newspapers until early March 1873, when fears were raised that unless progress was made, and quickly, donors might ask for their money back.

An editorial writer for the *Inquirer and Mirror* acknowledged another concern. Some opposed spending to honor the dead while "so many of the living are struggling with gaunt poverty, and some of them even in want of the necessities of life." But the editorial rejects such views, calling them arguments "ad captandum"—specious, unsound and designed to draw in the gullible. Honoring the dead, he believes, does not mean neglecting the living.

A week later, A.E.J., probably Arthur E. Jenks, celebrates that "The Blow Has Been Struck." A splendid design of the monument, he announces, can be seen in Mr. George W. Macy's store window. A.E.J. congratulates the previous week's editorial: "Your words will bear repeating: 'We shall not do the less for the living, because we pay our just debt of gratitude to the dead; nor will those who decline to do their duty in the one respect be the foremost to do it in the other.'"

The writer imagines the sounds of hammer and trowel betokening a speedy completion. He pictures a gala day when glad children in white "have wreaths and flowers in their hands," when martial music plays and flags wave in the summer air, a day when the thrilling news is sent abroad "that Nantucket has unveiled her Soldiers' Monument."

And the day was near.

ARRIVAL AND PLACEMENT

Within months, Churchill and Hitchcock received the order for the monument. On August 26, 1874, it arrived on the island aboard the schooner *A.O. Nettleton*. Until then, the town had dodged the question of where to erect it. The feeling seemed to be "let's *get* it first, and find a place for it afterwards."

On the day of arrival, a special town meeting authorized county commissioners "to procure and set off land where it will be placed." One suggestion was to remove the two-story "South School House" from its site on Orange Street and replace it with a "Monument Park." The schoolhouse, built in the 1850s, was thought by many "a prodigious elephant," too large for its purpose, inefficient, unsafe, unsightly and costly to maintain. A smaller school would be sufficient and town offices better placed closer to the town's center. The site's advantage for a monument was "a fine sea-view from the verge of the bank," making it visible to anyone entering the harbor. But this site was soon rejected. The schoolhouse may have been an "elephant," but it was still a useful elephant. Its removal would require building another schoolhouse that might cost more than retaining the old one. The South School House was saved and remained on Orange Street until 1931.

Realizing no location would be free of objections, the committee decided to place it "where the old town house and liberty-pole stood at the junction of Main and Milk Streets." The liberty pole had presumably been there since Revolutionary War times. Unfortunately, no illustration of it exists, but generally liberty poles were tall wooden poles with a "Phrygian cap" of the kind worn by Roman slaves at their top.

By October 10, 1874, the foundation wall was planted on the site. Several pieces of granite to form the structure had been hauled from the docks to where derricks would put them in their proper places. No derricks, however, were on the island, causing additional delay. Like so many other necessities, derricks needed to be brought from the mainland. As an *Inquirer and Mirror* writer observed, "We have no tools to work with, and everything must be imported. Had this job been put upon us during the palmy days of our commercial prosperity, we should have finished it ere this."

By the end of October, the monument was in place. The final cost was $3,252.85 (about $61,700 today), all but the town appropriation of $450 privately raised.

DEDICATION

In October 1874, the *Inquirer and Mirror* called for the monument to be completed "with a fitness and finish about all its surroundings which shall make it a credit to those who built it, as well as to the dead. Let it have an elaborate dedication, too, if the people really desire it; but this, in our view, is but a secondary matter, comparatively unimportant."

Much debate took place, pro and con, over the nature of a proper dedication but, according to the *Inquirer and Mirror*, with "no movement in the right direction." This changed as Decoration Day 1875 approached. Veterans of the war prepared, as every year, to honor their fallen comrades, "their brothers gone before." At the same time, some of the island's younger men determined to use the day to properly dedicate the monument.

In its column on the dedication ceremonies, the *Inquirer and Mirror* thanks the young men of the town "for their zeal and energy in the matter," at the same time criticizing "some of our older citizens [who] either from their non-patriotic feelings, or want of interest," failed to do so.

A special planning meeting at the Atheneum on May 17, 1875, had emphasized a dual purpose for Decoration Day: to "remember our dead, while we accord, as we ought, our gratitude to their surviving comrades in arms."

At an early hour on the day itself, Saturday, May 29, the monument was decorated with flowers, greenery and the American "ensign." Children of veterans arrived at the Unitarian church vestry before nine o'clock in the morning to be given floral bouquets. At nine, all participating in the procession to the monument had gathered in front of J.A. Cook's store on Main Street. First in line were the police, followed by musicians and then by Odd Fellows, soldiers' children, soldiers and the town's selectmen. They processed up Main Street to the monument where the children were grouped in a circle around it. Circled behind them were the surviving veterans of the war.

A special wreath of everlasting flowers and moss from Miss Martha Alley, then living in Lynne, was placed in front of the monument in honor of her brother Ferdinand Alley. A wreath to the rear had the initials "S.M.W. Jr." at its center for Shubael M. Winslow Jr.

The day was full of patriotic celebration. The children strewed flowers around the base of the monument. The first musical tribute was "Keller's American Hymn," a piece that failed to catch on during the war itself but

Civil War veterans, Memorial Day 1893. *Nantucket Historical Association.*

became popular after being featured in an 1872 Peace Festival. Its lyrics, though, are not particularly peaceful:

> *Foremost in battle, for Freedom to stand,*
> *We rush to arms when aroused by its call,*
> *Still as of yore when George Washington led,*
> *Thunders our war-cry, We conquer or fall!*

Reverend N.A. Haskell gave the oration. He asked the monument's granite blocks to "hold the memory of those whose names they bear as sacred as they are now held by the loving hearts throbbing here to-day. We have met to bid them repeat to coming ages the tale of their valor, their devotion, their consecration to a nation's welfare." Haskell quoted liberally from Lincoln's Gettysburg Address. Lincoln's words remained a feature of Decoration Day on Nantucket for many years to come.

Arthur E. Jenks read his poem "Our Soldiers' Monument" to an appreciative crowd. The poem paid tribute to the dead but was equally an appeal to pay heed to the living soldiers still in their midst:

> *I would not say,*
> *Leave no memorial. Let Sculpture tell*
> *Their valor's worth to the remotest day;*
> *But there's a duty to the living.*

After the closing hymn ("My Country, 'Tis of Thee) and the benediction, the soldiers "wended their way" to the North Cemetery, where part of the program seems to have been repeated.

It is now 140 years since Nantucket's Civil War Monument was dedicated in hopes that those on it would be remembered for what they gave their town and their country, which was no less than their lives. It may be time to remember that those on the monument were more than names.

5

More than Names:
The Men on the Monument

On Memorial Day 2014, the Nantucket Historical Association rang its ship's bell on the Whaling Museum's roof seventy-three times in memory of soldiers and sailors listed on the town's Civil War monument. The bell should have rung seventy-four times since seventy-four names are on the monument, not seventy-three. The miscount comes from George G. Worth's omission from an undated, alphabetical typed list of those on the monument, a list relied on as accurate for over twenty years. In this case, the last was also first. Worth would have been the last name on an alphabetical list. But he was also the first from Nantucket to die in the war and so is the first named on the monument.

Most on the monument are no longer remembered. Unless memories persist among their descendants—and many were young, unmarried and had no descendants—they are no more than names chiseled in granite, the context of their lives and deaths forgotten. Those who felt their loss and grieved them, who knew their stories, who had memories of their lives and deaths, are long gone. The Nantucket Historical Association possesses a handful of photographs of men in Civil War uniforms (and even one woman in her husband's uniform), but only a few. And some do not identify the person in the photograph.

No soldier or sailor who died after 1865 is included on the monument. Names on it are based almost entirely on lists of the dead published in the *Inquirer and Mirror*. The September 6, 1865 "In Memoriam" column held sixty-seven names and gave information on regiments, rank if above private for a

Monument Square, circa 1900. *Nantucket Historical Association.*

soldier or ordinary seaman for a sailor and ships served on, as well as date, place and cause of death, if known. On May 16, 1874, under the title "The Martyrs of the War," the *Inquirer and Mirror* added five names: Rufus Coffin, Edward P. Folger, Thomas Nevins, Charles B. Swain and Albert Kelley. John B. Coffin, previously described as missing, had been found and was dropped.

This was the newspaper's final list before the monument was erected. But the Monument Committee advised the public that it was open to further suggestions and asked its help in making the list of those honored "more correct." This led to dropping John D. Barnard, who appeared on all earlier lists, and adding Henry S. Folger, Charles R. Gruber, Peter C. Brook(s) and John Swain.

The first twenty-five names on the panel to the right of the dedicatory panel begins with George Worth. Of these, twenty-three died between October 21, 1861, and February 16, 1863. The final two, Henry S. Folger and Peter C. Brook (actually Brooks), are late additions. Folger was a member

GEORGE ? WORTH
ALBERT D. STACKPOLE
FREDERICK HOEC JR.
ARES M. HUNTER.
ALEXANDER BARKER.
CHARLES F. GREEN.
ALEXANDER P. MOORE.
WILLIAM K. SWAIN.
CHARLES B. SWAIN 3D.
WILLIAM H. WINSLOW.
GEORGE E. SNOW.
CHARLES A. MORRIS.
WILLIAM H. WILCOMB.
WILLIAM H. SWAIN.
EDWARD F. ALEXANDER.
EDWARD H. DAGGETT.
LEANDER F. ALLEY.
CLINTON SWAIN.
GEORGE K. ROBINSON.
CHARLES F. ELLIS.
CHARLES C. HOLMES.
GEORGE W. CHADWICK.
JOSEPH B. MOREY.
HENRY FOLGER.
PETER C. BROOK.

George Worth panel of the monument. *Mark White.*

of Company I, Twentieth Massachusetts Infantry. His death's relation to his service is unknown. Peter C. Brooks, who enlisted in Company H, Thirty-eighth Massachusetts, to the credit of Dartmouth, died of chronic diarrhea in Wareham, Massachusetts, on February 14, 1864.

Peter Brooks is not only non-chronological in date of death, he also violates a principle put forward in the May 16, 1874 "Martyrs of the War" column concerning "nonresidents" born on the island. The members of the Monument Committee admit the issue troubled them. Their decision, however, was that nonresidents "ought not, justly, to be counted here, as they are liable to be included in another list at the place where they enlisted." The Nantucket monument would bear fewer names if this practice had been followed, which it was not. At least ten on the monument enlisted as residents of towns other than Nantucket.

Nine on the first panel died of disease and fifteen in battle. In one case, death had little to do with service. Alexander P. Moore enlisted in Company H, Forty-fifth Massachusetts Infantry, on September 9, 1862. He was killed in a train accident a month later in Yarmouth, Massachusetts. As the *Inquirer and Mirror* described it:

> *In attempting to spring upon a car,* [he] *fell beneath it, and was so severely injured by the car passing over both legs, that he died at nine o'clock the same evening…Death on the battle field, would doubtless have been more welcome; but he had entered upon a soldier's life, and the honors of a soldier belong to his name.*

He was twenty-seven when he died and left a widow and three small children.

The second panel, to the left of the Main Street approach, begins with Acting Master James Folger, first from Nantucket to die serving in the navy. It ends with Charles R. Gruber, a late addition and another who violates the nonresident rule since he enlisted in New Bedford to the credit of Boston.

Of eight navy men on this panel, three died of battle injuries, the rest from disease. Henry G. Raymond may be a ninth navy man, but no military records have been found for him. According to the *Inquirer and Mirror*, he died on the hospital ship USS *Red Rover* off Mound City, Illinois. Since *Red Rover* was a Mississippi Squadron hospital ship, service in the navy is likely but not certain. Nor is it known whether his death came from battle or disease.

Rufus Coffin commanded the steamer *Flora*. He was an officer in the Revenue Service, not the navy.

Four soldiers on panel two died of disease, five were killed in battle or died from wounds and four died in Confederate prisons.

John F. Barnard, first to be listed on panel three, died on October 10, 1864, two days after being released from Salisbury Prison. Of twenty-four on panel three, thirteen were prisoners of war. Most probably succumbed

George Nelson Macy, who went from lieutenant to general in the Twentieth Massachusetts Infantry and survived the war. *Tinka Knopf family.*

to disease. Four soldiers who were not prisoners also died of illness, two others in battle and two from unknown causes. The four navy men here died of disease.

Last on the monument to die, though not last named, was Edward P. Folger. He enlisted in the Regular Army in late March 1865 with the war nearly over and died of "typho-malarial fever" in Mobile, Alabama, on December 7, 1865, just in time for inclusion on the monument. His effects were sent to his mother: one cap, one uniform coat, one pair of trousers, one cotton shirt and one woolen and one rubber blanket.

Eighty-one from Nantucket served in Company I, Twentieth Massachusetts Volunteer Infantry, called the Harvard Regiment because many of its officers were Harvard graduates. George Nelson Macy was working in Boston when the war began. As an officer in the Twentieth, he was responsible for recruiting volunteers. The natural place for him to do so was Nantucket, where he had grown up. Of the twenty-one he enlisted on July 18, 1861, seven died from battle or disease. One-third of the names on the monument are from Company I.

KILLED IN BATTLE

In the Battle of Ball's Bluff on October 21, 1861, the Twentieth and other regiments crossed to the Virginia side of the Potomac to check on

Confederate movements around Leesburg, Virginia. After climbing the steep bluff that gives the area its name, the men of Company I deployed with others on a field that backed up to the bluff. They soon discovered that the enemy was in force in front of them and their position untenable. Forced down the bluff, the Twentieth was caught between Confederates firing down at it from the bluff above and the Potomac River, which was the only avenue of escape. Boats, however, were in short supply, and many chose to swim across, including George Worth. Despite discovery of his body downstream days later with no obvious evidence of wounds, his friends believed him one of the many shot while trying to swim the river.

George Stackpole, eighteen years old, died five weeks later from a Minié ball wound to the groin. Albert Kelley also died but much later. One of 113 officers and men of the Twentieth taken prisoner and held in Richmond's Libby Prison, he died on Nantucket in August 1865. His death was attributed to illnesses contracted four years before in Libby Prison.

Clinton Swain, captain, Company D, Eighty-first Pennsylvania Infantry, killed at Fredericksburg. *Nantucket Historical Association.*

An even greater tragedy for the community of Nantucket was the Battle of Fredericksburg in December 1862. No company in the Twentieth was hit harder at Fredericksburg than the sixty men in Company I led by Henry Livermore Abbott. After crossing the Rappahannock River under enemy fire on December 11, Company I advanced into Fredericksburg with orders to push the Rebels back, street by street. William H. Winslow, Charles A. Morris, William H. Wilcomb and George E. Snow were killed outright. Charles F. Ellis, shot in the left ankle, died on January 19, 1863, of gangrene after his foot was amputated.

On December 13, the Twentieth was one of several

regiments ordered to attack Marye's Heights, a one-hundred-foot rise behind Fredericksburg where Confederate soldiers were entrenched behind stone walls. Macy, Abbott and others of the regiment knew an assault on the heights would be disastrous. It was. Nothing was gained, and three more from Nantucket were killed: Leander F. Alley and William H. Swain from the Twentieth and Clinton Swain, age twenty, who, four days earlier, had been promoted to captain in Company D, Eighty-first Pennsylvania Infantry.

Leander Alley was twenty-nine at the time of the battle. Promoted to first sergeant of Company I after Ball's Bluff, he had been promoted again to second lieutenant on August 29, 1862. At this promotion, both his men and the regiment's officers contributed to buy him the handsome sword now in the collection of the Nantucket Historical Association.

Henry Abbott wrote to Alley's mother on the day he died: "I can say from an intimate acquaintance with him, that he was as brave, resolute, and energetic, and at the same time as tender-hearted a man as I ever knew. When I first heard of his death (I didn't see

Leander F. Alley, Company I, Twentieth Massachusetts Infantry, a lieutenant when killed at Fredericksburg. *Nantucket Historical Association.*

Leander Alley's sword. *Nantucket Historical Association.*

him fall), I felt the same kind of pang as when I first heard of my brother's death, who was killed at Cedar Mountain."

Abbott wrote his sister a week later of the debacle at Fredericksburg and those responsible for it: "I firmly believe that…the men who ordered the crossing of the river are responsible to God for murder. I believe that Alley was just as much murdered as if he had been deliberately thrown into the river with a stone tied round his neck."

At Gettysburg on July 3, 1863, Company I was at the center of the Union line facing what came to be known as Pickett's charge. When a gap opened in Union defenses at a small copse to the right of the Twentieth, Abbott led his company in a fierce and successful fight to close it. Henry Jones, who claimed at enlistment to be eighteen (though he was actually fifteen), was mortally wounded in the head and died a few days later. Lieutenant Colonel George Nelson Macy, who survived the war, was one of several from Nantucket wounded. His left hand was hit by a Minié ball and was amputated.

Another from Nantucket probably killed at Gettysburg is not on the monument. Timothy Kelly, a thirty-nine-year-old Irishman, joined Company I in 1861 in the first wave of recruitment. After the battle, military records claimed he deserted at Gettysburg. Years later, however, his widow applied for a pension and received it, suggesting the Pension Bureau was persuaded that his disappearance at Gettysburg was due to death, not desertion.

The Twentieth engaged in most of the large battles fought in the East, including Cold Harbor. In later years, Ulysses S. Grant expressed regret for ordering the second assault at Cold Harbor on June 3, 1864, because "no advantage whatever was gained to compensate for the heavy loss we sustained." Two Nantucket soldiers died in that carnage: twenty-two-year-old George P. Chase of Company G, Tenth New York Infantry, and Ebenezer B. Gould, a Nantucket seaman who was probably forty-eight when he died fighting with Company A, Fifty-eighth Massachusetts Infantry.

After Cold Harbor, the Union was more hesitant about sending men into suicidal charges. When defenses at Petersburg proved impervious to assault, Grant laid siege to the city. During the siege, the Union army's efforts to sever railroad lines into Richmond led to skirmishes with Confederates defending them. Francis J. Rogers, a twenty-nine-year-old Nantucket blacksmith, was killed in such a fight a few weeks after mustering into Company H, Fifty-eighth Massachusetts Infantry.

William R. Beard, twenty-three and also a blacksmith, mustered into Company H with Rogers. His ability to buy his mother a house with his $325 enlistment bonus suggests how tempting financial rewards were for enlisting or reenlisting in the war's later years. Two weeks after his friend Francis Rogers was killed, Beard was one of the unfortunate soldiers captured at the Battle of the Crater on July 30, 1864, a military disaster that followed the successful explosion of a mine under Petersburg's defenses. Grant called it "the saddest affair I have witnessed in this war." Untrained Union soldiers charged into the crater instead of around it, making them targets for Confederate soldiers firing from the rim. Over 500 were killed outright, almost 2,000 wounded and another 1,413 reported missing or captured. In Beard's regiment, 84 were captured. Beard was one of them. According to Nathan Downey, a Company H sergeant imprisoned with him, Beard was wounded in the battle and died on September 2, 1864, in Poplar Lawn Hospital in Petersburg.

Augustus D. Briggs, Company A, Third Massachusetts Cavalry, was mortally wounded on October 19, 1864, in the Battle of Cedar Creek, the final battle for control of the Shenandoah Valley. He died on November 14, 1864, in the National Hospital in Baltimore. The total personal effects sent to his wife were a pocketknife, a pair of gloves and a pocket book.

The last Nantucket man to die in actual battle was Shubael M. Winslow Jr., twenty-one years old and a shoemaker when he enlisted in Company E, Tenth Massachusetts Infantry, on June 21, 1861, two months after Fort Sumter. When the Tenth disbanded as a regiment on June 20, 1864, Winslow and others from the Tenth transferred into Company I of the Thirty-seventh Massachusetts Infantry. At that time, he listed his residence as Springfield.

Shubael Winslow fought through the entire war.

Unknown soldier in Civil War uniform, "a cousin of Judith Winslow (Hill)." *Nantucket Historical Association.*

He enlisted as it began and was mortally wounded at the final assault on Petersburg on April 2, 1865, seven days before Lee's surrender to Grant at Appomattox. He died on April 24, 1865. Winslow's widow, Anna, remarried in 1868. Her new husband had also fought from the beginning of the war to the end but survived. He was Benjamin B. Pease, a captain in the Massachusetts Twentieth when he mustered out on June 1, 1865.

Among the Nantucket Historical Association's photographs of Nantucket soldiers and sailors is one sent in January 1926 by F.H. Hill of Utica, New York, with the note "A cousin of Judith Winslow (Hill) A soldier of the Civil War and a resident of Nantucket, at that time." He adds: "I cannot recall his name."

Shubael Winslow and William Winslow (who was killed at Fredericksburg) were cousins of Judith Winslow. One or the other, or perhaps a cousin with a different name, is the soldier in the photo.

KILLED AT SEA

As the Civil War began, the U.S. Navy's fleet numbered 42 commissioned ships and 48 not in service. By war's end, 671 ships sailed for the Union. This huge increase required equal but temporary increases in officers and men. Of fourteen Nantucket men who died while serving in the Union navy, four were "acting" officers at their rank.

Acting Master James Folger was killed while serving on the bark USS *Roebuck* on blockade duty off the coast of Florida. He had been ordered to investigate contraband cotton being loaded on a Confederate blockade runner. Guerrillas attacked his landing party, causing heavy losses. Folger was wounded in the leg, leading to its amputation and his death. He died on April 15, 1863, at sea aboard the *Roebuck*.

On October 29, 1861, Frederick Andrews, twenty-seven, was serving as an ordinary seaman on the USS *Pawnee* near Port Royal, South Carolina, when it was struck by a cannonball that splintered the wheelhouse and wounded Andrews. He died from his wounds in Nantucket in early 1863.

David Morrow, forty, was killed on August 6, 1864, aboard the USS *Hartford* at the Battle of Mobile Bay. The *Hartford* was Admiral David Farragut's flagship, and it was in this battle that he made his famous call of "Damn the torpedoes!" as he sailed into the bay's heavily mined waters. Of those in the Union fleet, 150, including David Morrow, died in the Battle of Mobile Bay.

Admiral David Farragut's flagship, the USS *Hartford*. David Morrow died while serving on it. *Naval History and Heritage Command.*

Howard Vincent, age twenty, also came to grief in a minefield. He was serving on the USS *Commodore Jones* patrolling the James River when it was hit by "an electrically fired mine" on May 6, 1864, killing him.

DEATH FROM DISEASE

More soldiers and sailors died of disease than injuries in the Civil War. Infectious diseases—dysentery, typhoid, pneumonia, malaria, smallpox—devastated soldiers and sailors in both the North and the South, in camps, on ships and in prisons.

First on the monument to die of disease was Frederick Hoeg Jr., age fifty-two. Hoeg belonged to Company K of the Seventy-fourth New York Infantry. He died of pneumonia at Park Barracks, New York City. According to the Barney Genealogical Record, he was returning from the war at the time, presumably to Nantucket.

Two on the monument died within days of each other in Baltimore. Charles F. Green, a nineteen-year-old farmer, died from an unnamed "disease" on July 11, 1862, six months after enlisting in Company C, Eighteenth Massachusetts Infantry. Two days later, in the same city, Corporal

Alexander Barker of Company F, Twenty-second Massachusetts Infantry, died of typhoid fever.

At least ten Nantucket recruits were disabled, some permanently, on the 1862 march from Antietam to Harpers Ferry and then on to a bitterly cold encampment on Bolivar Heights. In an 1892 pension deposition, George A. Backus, who survived the war, described the post-Antietam march: "Antietam was our first battle and after it we were marched down to Harpers Ferry where we forded the [river] and went on to camp on Bolivar Heights wet and cold and a great many of us took colds and had a severe camp diarrhea and some of the boys died with it." Lack of blankets increased the suffering in the cold of Bolivar Heights. Many new recruits of the Twentieth had thrown their blankets away on the hot march from Alexandria, Virginia, to Antietam.

William K. Swain and George W. Chadwick, both nineteen, died soon after the march, Swain a month later from typhoid fever and Chadwick several months later from dysentery. With the help of a friend, Chadwick wrote to his family that he was much encouraged by his doctor's telling him "that I will get along very well…and as soon as I am able he will discharge me." He died the next day.

Corporal Charles S. Russell, Company H, Forty-fifth Massachusetts Volunteer Militia, died of typhoid fever in Beaufort, South Carolina. *Nantucket Historical Association.*

In August 1862, President Lincoln tried to attract 300,000 new recruits by creating regiments with nine-month tours of duty. The appeal inspired the song "We Are Coming Father Abraham, 300,000 Strong." The Forty-fifth Massachusetts was one of these nine-month units. Company H included 55 servicemen from Nantucket.

The Forty-fifth's main encampment was in the area of Newbern, North Carolina. Charles C. Holmes, a forty-two-year-old seaman, and Joseph B.

Morey, a thirty-two-year-old farmer, died of fever there in January 1863. Charles S. Russell, twenty-three, a Nantucket carpenter, died of typhoid fever on June 17, 1863, in Beaufort, South Carolina, just days before the Forty-fifth embarked from Beaufort for Boston to end its tour of duty.

The Nantucket Historical Association has in its collection a photograph identified as that of Corporal Charles S. Russell. Elsewhere, the same image carries the name Charles Crocker. Crocker, however, was a private. Russell was a corporal. Since the person in the image has a corporal's insignia on his sleeve, he is probably Russell.

Charles B. Swain, a saddler in Company K, First Massachusetts Cavalry, also died in Beaufort in 1862, probably of typhoid fever.

Sailors were not immune to illness. Three, all sons of whaling captains, are on panel two. Ferdinand W. Defriez (DeFriez on the monument) and Henry C. Russell were twenty-nine when they died on the same day, September 22, 1863, Defriez from "hemorrhage of the lungs," Russell of yellow fever. Ferdinand Alley, a cousin of Leander Alley, died of consumption at a naval hospital in Brooklyn in 1864.

George G. Coffin, a thirty-five-year-old acting ensign serving in the West Gulf Squadron, died of yellow fever on October 11, 1864, aboard the gunboat *Owasco* off Galveston, Texas.

Rufus Coffin also died as a result of disease. In 1861, Coffin was commissioned

Acting Ensign George G. Coffin, who died on the gunboat *Owasco* of yellow fever. *Nantucket Historical Association.*

a first lieutenant in the Revenue Marine Service, a service established in 1790 to combat smuggling and enforce tariff laws. As such, it belonged to the Department of the Treasury. President Lincoln and Secretary of the Treasury Salmon P. Chase both signed Coffin's commission papers. Less than six months after enlisting, however, Coffin was reported to the treasury for disobeying orders. Secretary Chase outlined the charges against Coffin in a letter to him as "delaying the departure of the steamer *Flora* under your command and destined for Port Royal," charges so grave "that I deemed it my duty to relieve you of the command of that vessel, and to direct you to report to the Collector of New York for trial."

In this May 29, 1862 letter, Chase goes on to absolve Coffin of any fault. In fact, he praises him for "the successful navigation of the Steamer 'Flora' to Port Royal, built as she was for internal navigation only," which gave "evidence of nautical skill and judgement [*sic*] highly gratifying to the Department."

Port Royal, however, was not a fortunate port for Rufus Coffin. In an 1881 pension application for his widow, Winnifred, he is described as contracting "Southern fever at Port Royal, S.C., which produced paralysis of the brain from which he died at Taunton Insane Hospital on tenth day of August, 1863." Misfortune did not end there. The application describes Coffin as a lieutenant in the "navy" when he died. But he was not. He was in the U.S. Revenue Marine service. The Bureau of Pensions rejected the pension request, "as there is no law allowing the widow of a Revenue Cutter officer, a pension."

PRISONERS OF WAR

Capture by the enemy often proved deadly in the notorious conditions of Civil War prison camps. Men died of starvation, exposure and of all the diseases found where overcrowded and unsanitary conditions exist.

When "Adelbert" Kelley mustered into Company I of the Twentieth Massachusetts in 1861, he preferred to be known as Albert. He is only "Adelbert" in his birth records and on the Civil War monument. Although he died in 1865 and so is listed on the third panel, Kelley was among the first Nantucket soldiers taken prisoner and one whose death years later directly related to his earlier captivity. Taken prisoner at Ball's Bluff on October 21, 1861, he was released on December 15, 1861. Kelley returned to Company I but was sick much of the time and eventually discharged for disability. The

Nantucket doctor caring for him in 1865 quoted Kelley as saying that "he hardly knew what it was like to be sick until he went into the army and while there [he suffered from] want of proper care and nourishment in Rebel prison [and] broke down and had never seen a well day since."

Dozens of Nantucket veterans suffered aftereffects similar to Kelley's. Crippled, feeble, often with chronic diarrhea, rheumatic diseases and debilitating wounds, many lived for years in great distress. Kelley died on August 28, 1865, in Nantucket, two years after being mustered out of Company I of the Twentieth. If he had died four months later, his name also would not be on the monument.

Two Nantucket members of Company M, Second Massachusetts Cavalry, were captured on February 22, 1864, with sixty-eight other men in Dranesville, Virginia, when their company was ambushed by troops belonging to Mosby's Rangers. Both their names are incorrect on the monument. Edward P. Hamblen should be "Hamblin," and Alvin C. Coffin is actually Alvin R. Coffin. Both died at Andersonville Prison in Georgia: Hamblin on June 9, 1864, and Coffin of dysentery on August 9, 1864, after an illness of "about one month."

Charles H. Raymond of Company I also died at Andersonville. Wounded at Antietam, he deserted at Gettysburg. Court-martialed, he was sentenced to prison in the Dry Tortugas for the time remaining in his service. Instead, he was allowed to return to the army and was with his company in 1864. Taken prisoner during the Wilderness Campaign (May 5–6, 1864), he died at Andersonville on June 12, 1864, according to military records. Andersonville Cemetery records, however, give March 14 as his death date, well before the Battle of the Wilderness.

Of the twenty-five on the monument's third panel, thirteen became prisoners of war, most around the time Ulysses S. Grant discontinued prisoner exchanges. Grant reasoned that released Southern soldiers would return to the fight against the North, which prolonged the war. "It is hard on our men held in Southern prisons not to exchange them," he wrote, "but it is humanity to those left in the ranks to fight our battles. Every man we hold, when released on parole or otherwise, becomes an active soldier against us at once either directly or indirectly."

Benjamin Smith, a forty-three-year-old Nantucket seaman, mustered into Company H, Fifty-eighth Massachusetts Infantry, on April 18, 1864. He was a late enlistee with a wife and two young children. On July 30, 1864, the Fifty-eighth was one of the regiments in the disastrous charge into the crater at Petersburg. Smith and eighty-three others from his regiment were taken

Seth Chase, Company I, Thirty-ninth Massachusetts Infantry, died as a result of being a prisoner of war. *Nantucket Historical Association.*

prisoner and put in one of six converted warehouses in Danville, Virginia. Smith died of disease in Danville on November 6, 1864.

After the failed assault on the crater, Union efforts turned to isolating Petersburg. The first target for this was the Wheldon Railroad that connected Petersburg with the South's last port in Wilmington, North Carolina. In the battle for the railroad on August 18, 1864, Seth Chase, a thirty-two-year-old former mariner, was captured. Exchanged on March 10, 1865, he died in Nantucket on April 3, 1865.

August 25, 1864, was another cruel day for the Twentieth Massachusetts. The Twentieth had also been sent to destroy rail tracks used to supply Petersburg. During the fight at Reams Station, Virginia, Confederate soldiers surrounded the men of the Twentieth. Their only option was to surrender, which they did. Five officers were captured and imprisoned. They all survived. Enlisted men were less fortunate. Of the ninety-nine taken prisoner, twenty-five died, most at Salisbury Prison in North Carolina. Five of the prisoners were from Nantucket: John Barnard, Arthur Rivers, Sam Crocker, Edward Randall and Benjamin B. Pease. Pease, the only officer in the group, was also the only one to survive.

John F. Barnard, a Nantucket fireman, had reenlisted one month before being taken captive. His jailers released him on October 8, 1864, and he died two days later. According to the *Nantucket Weekly Mirror*, "Fountain Engine Co. No. 8 displayed their flag at half-mast as a token of respect for their deceased member."

Arthur M. Rivers was fifteen when he enlisted in 1862 but, like many men too young to serve, claimed to be older. Hospitalized for five months after the hard march from Antietam in 1862, he returned to Company I in time for Gettysburg, where he was seriously wounded. Despite that, he reenlisted in February 1864. When he died of chronic diarrhea at Salisbury, he was seventeen years old.

Samuel C. Crocker also died at Salisbury. Like Rivers, he added to his age in order to enlist. Wounded at Chancellorsville and Spotsylvania, he died of pneumonia in the prison hospital at Salisbury on January 31, 1865.

Edward (Ned) Randall does not appear in the Barney Genealogical Record of Nantucket families or in Nantucket birth records. He joined Company I without specifying a place of residence. For occupation, he listed "Drummer." He enlisted on July 19, 1862; reenlisted on February 17, 1864; and was promoted to corporal a few months later.

Writing his parents shortly after he was taken prisoner, Arthur Rivers described what had happened and who from Nantucket was captured with him: "Our whole Regiment was captured on the 25 of Aug. There is Ned Randall John Barnard Sam Crocker Lieut Pease of Nantu." Randall was clearly part of the Nantucket group. The Confederates sent him first to Libby Prison and then to Salisbury, but he was in Richmond again, probably in Libby Prison, when he died of disease on March 2, 1865. The bodies of Barnard, Rivers and Crocker were returned to Nantucket for final burial. Ned Randall is buried in the Richmond National Cemetery.

Libby Prison, Richmond, Virginia. *National Archives.*

William P. (not R. as on the monument) Kelley was also a member of Company I, Twentieth Massachusetts. Kelley was captured at Spotsylvania in 1864. In his *Memoir of Service in the Civil War*, Josiah Fitch Murphy described Kelley as captured when a group of Confederates showed a flag of truce and men of Company I went to the breastworks to take prisoners. They soon realized only half the Southerners in the area had surrendered. "The other half immediately began firing and Kelley with the rest who were on the breastworks had to jump down inside to save their lives." Captured on May 12, 1864, Kelley was paroled on February 26, 1865, and died two weeks later in Wilmington, Delaware.

The John Swain Mystery

One whose story was almost lost is John Swain, the last name on the monument. Numerous John Swains appear in town and Barney Genealogical records but none whose dates fit for inclusion on the monument. No military records for him have been discovered, nor does his name appear in contemporary *Inquirer and Mirror* lists of soldiers and sailors.

Past efforts to identify him have failed. For example, James Grieder suggested John T. Swain of Tilsbury because of his service in Company H, Forty-fifth Massachusetts Infantry, a company and regiment in which many Nantucketers served. But many from Tilsbury also served in it, and John T. Swain was born and died (after the war) in Tilsbury.

Swain's is one of four names added between the May 16, 1874 "Martyrs of the War" listing and the monument's erection in October 1874. Someone responded to the Monument Committee's invitation to suggest others deserving a place on the monument with the name of John Swain. But who is John Swain?

A John Swain died in Nantucket on April 25, 1865. The April 29 *Inquirer and Mirror* published the following death notice:

In this town, on Tuesday last, John Swain, a native of Lahaina, aged 46 years.
Happy soul, thy days are ended,
All thy mourning days below,
Go, by angel guard attended,
To the right of Jesus go.

Final panel with John Swain as the last name. *Mark White.*

Nothing is said here about service in the military. But this John Swain is likely the one on the monument. To begin with, he was in the military. He is listed in an *Inquirer and Mirror* column of June 8, 1901, "Where Rest the Soldier and Sailor Dead," that identifies where on the island soldiers and sailors of the Civil War were buried. John Swain is one of two Civil War veterans listed as in the colored cemetery (now officially the "coloured" cemetery). The date of death on his tombstone is the same as the John Swain who was a native of Lahaina: April 25, 1865.

Left: John Swain's gravestone in the Nantucket Coloured Cemetery. *Mark White.*

Below: Members of Nantucket's Grand Army of the Republic, Thomas M. Gardner Post, 1890s. *Nantucket Historical Association.*

Edouard Stackpole in "Nantucket's Gallant Men in Blue of the Civil War" (*Inquirer and Mirror*, June 5, 1942) specifies Swain's service: "Sampson Pompey and John Swain became two of Nantucket's colored men enlisting in the Navy."

The Hawaiian John Swain was a Nantucket resident in the navy and died in time for inclusion. His lack of service records or a known service-related death is not unique for the monument. No service-related death is recorded for Henry S. Folger, and no military records are discoverable for Henry G. Raymond. As a member of the colored community, it may not be surprising that John Swain was one of the last to be suggested for placement on the monument. Perhaps Sampson Pompey, who joined the navy with him, suggested his friend be added at the time the final call went out for names to be honored.

John Swain is probably Hawaiian and not African American, but with John Swain among them, the seventy-four on the Nantucket memorial are no longer all white.

Three African Americans—George Michaels, Hiram Reed and Sampson Pompey—belonged to the Thomas M. Gardner Post 207, Grand Army of the Republic. They can be seen sitting together in a group photograph probably taken around the time the GAR reestablished on Nantucket in 1891.

A NOTE ON NAMES

A few names on the monument differ from military and Barney records, suggesting how closely names on the monument follow spellings in the *Inquirer and Mirror*'s lists. The "In Memoriam" list of September 6, 1865, gives Seth C. Chace, Edward Hamblen and William R. Kelley, not the Seth C. Chase, Edward P. Hamblin and William P. Kelley they themselves used in enlisting and that are found in the Barney records. Such changes could seem insignificant. Chace and Chase sound alike, Ps and Rs are similar in shape, Hamblens exist in the world as well as Hamblins (though no "Hamblens" appear in the Barney records, only Hamblins).

The case of Alvin R. and Alvin C. Coffin is different. The monument lists Alvin C. Coffin. The soldier who served in Company M, Second Massachusetts Cavalry, was Alvin R. Coffin. By 1860, he was married to Catherine E. Morey of West Bridgewater, Massachusetts, and living with her parents in West Bridgewater. In a deposition supporting a pension for his widow, Catherine, David J. Folger gave testimony: "That on the ninth day of August last past he is knowing to the fact of the death in Andersonville Prison after about one month's sickness from Dysentery of private Alvin R. Coffin formerly of this place [Nantucket] but latterly of West Bridgewater of this state." In military records and throughout the lengthy pension records, he is Alvin R. Coffin.

Alvin R. Coffin is also misidentified as Alvin C. Coffin in the Barney records but with the correct parents, James M. Coffin and Anna J. Swain. The Barney record describes him as "single" when he dies at "Richmond Prison." He was in fact married. There is another Alvin C. Coffin born in 1836 in the Barney records who does not seem to have been in the military and was single during the war. He died in 1870.

The confusion over the name and marital status of Alvin R. Coffin appears related to his having left the island. Alvin R. Coffin no longer lived in Nantucket when the war began. The news of his marriage did not reach Eliza Starbuck Barney. By 1870, four years before the monument became a reality, his father and his father's second wife (his mother died in 1839) were already far away in Kankakee, Illinois, where James M. Coffin eventually died in 1880. The Monument Committee simply followed the *Inquirer and Mirror*'s listing of Alvin C. Coffin. But it was Alvin R. Coffin who should be honored on the monument.

The list is not perfect. Some were left off accidentally or on the principle not usually followed that nonresidents not be included. One left off was Nantucket-born Charles G. Macy, who was a resident of New Bedford when he enlisted in Company I, Eighteenth Massachusetts Infantry. Captured on May 5, 1864 at the Battle of the Wilderness, he died at Andersonville prison on September 1, 1864. Date and place of death are in the Barney Genealogical Record, but unlike others born in Nantucket and enlisted as residents of other towns, he is not on the monument.

Allen Bacon, however, is. Bacon was a member of Company H, Forty-fifth Massachusetts Infantry. In the *Inquirer and Mirror* list of September 6, 1865, he is in the group under 1863: "Allen Bacon, missing since Dec.—last heard from at camp on Riker's Island." Military records, however, have him mustering out of the Forty-fifth with others of his unit on July 7, 1863, and surviving the war.

The Forty-fifth embarked for Newbern, North Carolina, on November 5, 1862. What Bacon may have been doing at a camp on Riker's Island is unclear. There seems to be no Riker's Island in North Carolina. There is one in New York, but the Forty-fifth was not there in December 1862, and Riker's Island was not a war zone. The Forty-fifth was on its Goldsboro expedition, which led to the Battle of Kinston.

Only twenty from the Forty-fifth died in battle, including Edward H. Daggett and George K. Robinson at Kinston. Twenty-seven were lost from disease, accident or having gone missing. Of these twenty-seven, four were from Nantucket. Alexander P. Moore died in a railway accident in Yarmouth and Charles C. Holmes, Joseph B. Morey and Charles S. Russell of disease in the Carolinas. Alan Bacon is not in these lists, nor is anything heard of him after he is described in official records as "mustering out" on July 7, 1863.

But if he does not deserve to be on the monument, would not someone from Nantucket in Company H of the Forty-fifth have had him removed before the monument went up? Charles D. Barnard, who was on both the September 6, 1865 and May 16, 1874 lists and thought "killed in entrenchments near Richmond, June 11, 1862," was removed at the last minute because he was very much alive. He lived into the twentieth century. John B. Coffin, listed as "missing" in 1862, was found and also removed. But Allen Bacon stayed on.

One can only wonder…why?

6

The Industrial Revolution
on Nantucket

S mokestacks and factories do not seem associated in any way with Nantucket today with its fresh air, clean beaches and quaint downtown streets and docks. But visitors to Nantucket during the heyday of whaling would have found a much different waterfront ringed by sooty factories, warehouses and workshops based on the dirty business of converting whales into usable products. It was decidedly not picturesque. As with all working ports, it would not have been difficult for a hardworking sailor to find a seedy bar or a brothel in which to spend his money.

When the whaling era came to an end, Nantucket looked to the Industrial Revolution to replace whaling. Various manufacturing enterprises were started, some of which resulted in cheap mass-produced goods, something else that does not easily come to mind when thinking about the island today with its expensive handicrafts and boutiques.

Nantucket was well suited to the whaling industry until the advent of the railroads, and between 1815 and 1848, over eight hundred whaling ships left Nantucket Harbor. Whaling employed many people on both land and sea. In the mid-1840s, it was estimated that over 1,100 Nantucket men were employed in the land-based industries that supported the hundreds more who sailed to hunt whales.

Recalling those times in 1880 for a column in the *Inquirer and Mirror* about the "old days," an unnamed author wrote, "There was work for every man then who wanted to work, and when the old South bell rung out the hour of noon, Main Street, as well as the other streets leading up from the wharves,

Whaling ship *Sarah* of Nantucket, circa 1850s, probably docked in New Bedford. *Nantucket Historical Association.*

were filled with an army of workingmen, going up for their dinners, presenting a sight, the like of which I fear we shall never look upon again."

As whaling flourished and ships got larger, it was big business just to outfit the ships, and the "army" of workers increased.

Every ship required dozens of masts and spars, sails, miles of rope, dozens of oak casks, hundreds of oak blocks, hundreds of tools and weapons used in hunting and in cutting up whales, in addition to the outfitting and building of the smaller boats used to chase the whales in the famous Nantucket sleigh rides. Whaling voyages took years, and ships needed sufficient supplies to feed and clothe their crews, as well as materials to make repairs at sea, far from ports. And when the ships returned to the island, tons of whale oil had to be processed into candles and refined oil and made ready to ship off island, requiring more casks and boxes. Today, many of the items involved in the business of whaling are on display at Nantucket's Whaling Museum.

There are only two accounts in Nantucket's *Inquirer* that provide an overview of the many industries and enterprises that existed on the island during the whaling era, but from these accounts, it is possible to get a general idea of its scope. One account is from 1832, and the other is from 1855. The first describes the whaling industry slightly before whaling reached its height on the island, and the second describes the state of the industries as whaling was in decline.

Although the majority of large whaling ships were built off island, a few were built on Nantucket, including the *Charles Caroll*, a ship of 376 tons that was built at Brant Point in 1832. The smaller boats lowered to chase individual whales were more likely to have been built locally. By 1855, there were still four boat builders on the island that built ninety-nine boats that year. One such boat shop, called The Big Shop, is now a residence located on the corner of Milk Street and Quaker Road.

The business of whaling required a good deal of skilled carpentry. Masts and spars spawned a completely separate industry. Each ship needed at least twenty-five different spars. Generally made of heartwood, each spar had to be cut, rounded, shaped and fitted for individual ships. It is not clear how many spar manufacturers there were on Nantucket over the years, but in 1832, there were four. In 1855, eighty-nine spars and masts were made on island.

In addition to spars and masts, ships needed wooden blocks of a variety of sizes, most used to fasten ropes. In 1832, there were two block

Whale oil barrels being unloaded on Nantucket, circa 1910. *Nantucket Historical Association.*

factories on the island. None were reported in 1855, an indication of whaling's decline.

Whaling also required a huge number of various shapes and sizes of wooden barrels, buckets and casks. Manufacturing them was a large and lucrative business. Casks and barrels were used to store supplies, including flour and water. Huge casks, usually made of white oak, were needed to store whale oil. Coopers were skilled carpenters who learned to shape the wood into strong, usually flat-bottomed vessels rimmed with iron. Many of the containers had to be air- and/or watertight so that whatever was stored would not spoil. In the 1830s, there were an astonishing twenty-two cooperages on Nantucket manufacturing thousands of wooden containers. Recollecting those shops in the 1880s, it was written:

Coopers' shops were having full swing all over town. The making of harpoons, lances, spades, knives and the thousand-and-one articles taken away on our whalers, kept a large force always at work. Their shops were as a general thing strung along the street, just at the head of the wharves, and were mostly low, dingy-looking buildings, but were lighted up within by the bright fires from the forges.

Cooperage at 6 Vestal Street in the 1880s. *Nantucket Historical Association.*

Whale ships required miles of rope. Nantucket had ten ropewalks where rope was made from the tons of hemp delivered from off island. Ropewalks employed over three hundred people during the heyday of whaling. Rope making is difficult to envision, as ropewalks no longer exist. The work was hard, dangerous and dirty. Workers breathed in fibers that hung in the air, and ropewalks were susceptible to fire from the highly flammable hemp. The machinery that stretched and twisted the fibers was capable of taking off fingers and arms. As the name conjures, men had to walk the rope the length of the long buildings, looping strands to make rope long enough to anchor a ship or to attach to harpoons long enough to fasten to whales as they dove deep attempting to escape.

Ropewalks manufactured a huge variety of widths and lengths of rope, from slender fishing lines to huge, twisted strands strong enough to hold heavy anchors or to bind several tons of whales to the sides of ships before they were cut up. Mystic Seaport in Connecticut has preserved a segment of the Plymouth Cordage Company's ropewalk. While the building seems long at 250 feet, the museum has preserved only one-fourth of the original ropewalk.

Where all the Nantucket ropewalks were located is not now known. One was on North Beach Street, one between Union and Washington Streets, one on Brant Point and one on Milk Street by Prospect Hill Cemetery. A fire in 1838 originated in a downtown ropewalk owned by Joseph James on Union Street. From there, the fire spread to over twenty buildings, destroying at least three candle factories.

In January 1839, a new "improved" ropewalk was opened on Brant Point. The newspaper noted the wisdom of locating it "away from the town" because of the hazard of fire. The 860-foot-long structure generated pride for being such a "commanding object" as ships rounded Brant Point. The new company employed "Mr. James, the unfortunate sufferer in the late fire," to manage the operations. It was the first ropewalk on the island to use a ten-horsepower steam engine to assist in the making of rope. The new ropewalk could make cables $66\frac{1}{2}$ fathoms long in just one day. (This is over 400 feet long.) The factory turned more than a ton of hemp into rope every week. The editor noted that it was a "delight" to witness the "improvements of the present age" and praised the forty "respectable, orderly and credible" men who worked in the modern facility.

There were also several sail lofts making and repairing the many sails required by the sailing ships. Every ship needed 20 to 30 sails in a variety of sizes, totaling over an acre of sailcloth. It was skilled work; each sail had to be carefully measured, cut and sewn. An apprenticeship of at least three

Tryworks and other tools made for whaling in Sanderson Hall, the Nantucket Whaling Museum. *Nantucket Historical Association*

years was necessary before a man was considered a master sail maker. Sail lofts required large open spaces to accommodate the yards of cotton needed to make huge mainsails. In the 1830s, there were four sail lofts on the island, and over twenty years later, there were still three. In 1855, even as whaling was in decline, those three lofts made 202 sails.

Blacksmiths were also busy equipping whale ships, and Nantucket's smithies imported tons of iron every year. A huge array of metal implements were required to fit up a ship—hinges, cleats and anchor chains, to name a few. More specialized tools were required to hunt the whales, including harpoons and lances. Once a whale was caught, specific instruments were used to cut and process the whale from its head to its tail. At its peak, there were about a dozen blacksmith shops on the island, most clustered around the wharves. Thirty-six tons of iron was processed into implements for the ships leaving Nantucket in 1855, indicating the importance of the industry, even as whaling was waning.

Whale oil was processed at sea by onboard tryworks, but the oil was refined when it got back to Nantucket. Transforming oil into candles and

Former candle factory, circa 1880, at a corner of Pine and High Streets. *Nantucket Historical Association.*

refined oil was one of the biggest auxiliary industries associated with whaling. Nantucket's oil, considered the best in the world, lit the street lamps of cities from New York to London. The first candle factory on Nantucket was built in 1772, and during the height of whaling, over four million candles left Nantucket every year. At that time, Nantucket had seventeen oil factories and nineteen candle factories, plus two more factories devoted solely to making boxes for the candles. Nantucket's Whaling Museum is housed in the former Hadwen and Barney Candle Factory, where visitors can learn more about the once-lucrative business of turning whale oil into light.

As the Industrial Revolution unfolded and whaling declined, it was natural that Nantucket turned to other kinds of factories as a way to bolster its sagging economy. Already familiar with manufacturing items for ships, it made sense that Nantucket would embrace the new methods of mass production. However, the factories built on the island between the era of whaling and the era of tourism were not particularly successful. Most went out of business after a few years. The major problem entrepreneurs faced was the cost of transporting raw material to the island and shipping finished products to the mainland. Cities with access to the railroads had a clear advantage. Nevertheless, there were valiant efforts to bring industrialization to the island to rescue the flagging economy.

One of the first industries not related to whaling involved silk. In the mid-1830s, silk was all the rage in the fashion world. Once the exclusive domain of the Chinese, there was huge demand for the luxurious fabric. Along the eastern seaboard, there was wild speculation in silk manufacturing, and several enterprising Nantucketers decided to give it a try. Abolitionists also encouraged the silk business as a way to avoid slave-produced cotton. Nantucket businessmen first invested in mulberry trees upon which silkworms feed, hoping the trees would thrive on the island. The first recorded planting was in 1832, when William H. Gardner planted a mulberry tree in Quaise. Soon other mulberry trees were planted, including 120 trees at the town's asylum for the poor in Quaise. Mulberry trees were planted in town on Academy Hill and on North Water Street. The largest grove of 4,000 trees was at Aaron Mitchell's farm in Polpis.

Silk strands were spun into material. Tree growers Gardner and Mitchell financed the Atlantic Silk Factory in late 1835, building their factory at 10–12 Gay Street. In fact, the street is named for Gamaliel Gay, the Rhode Island inventor who designed the silk-making machinery and oversaw the building of the Nantucket factory with its sixteen-horsepower engine. Wastewater was dumped into a small pond across the street. The factory had four

Atlantic Silk Factory building today at 10–12 Gay Street. *Mark White.*

twelve-foot-long spinning machines, each with five hundred bobbins. The six looms produced fifty thousand linen coats and thousands of vests and handkerchiefs in its eight years of operation. While the industries associated with whaling depended on men, it was women who provided the bulk of the labor in silk manufacturing, and approximately fifty women were hired to run the machines of the Atlantic Silk Factory.

To further encourage the silk industry, Massachusetts authorized a one-dollar bounty for every ten pounds of silkworm cocoons and another dollar for every reel of silk. On a visit to the island in 1836, Governor Edward Everett toured Nantucket's silk factory and praised the industrious Nantucketers, "whether in seizing the fibers of the silkworm, or in waging wars with the monsters of the deep—may they be equally prosperous."

In its early years, the silk industry was successful, and in 1836, Nantucket's silk products were shown at an exhibit at the American Institute in New York City. It was reported that "Nantucket's articles are of superior fabric and manufacture," and that, if the island could produce silk in large quantities, the island's silk would "soon supplant all silk goods from France or India."

It was not, however, to be. The mulberry trees failed to thrive in the island's sandy soil. Although a few sturdy survivors can still be found, most of the trees died. The silk factory closed its doors in 1844, its machinery moved to the second floor of Aaron Mitchell's warehouse. The machinery's weight eventually caused the warehouse to collapse, destroying everything inside. It was the end of Nantucket's foray into silk making.

Nantucket also turned to shoe and boot manufacturing, and several shoe and boot factories were started. In 1855, one such factory produced 1,150 pairs of boots and almost 5,000 pairs of shoes. It was, however, a small venture, employing only eleven men and twenty women, and it did not stay in business for long.

Other boot and shoe factories opened in 1859. The Nantucket Boot and Shoe Company was owned by E.F. Alley and an off-island investor. Located on the second floor of a building in the Coffin block of stores on Main Street, it employed sixty men. Albert Swain also had a small factory that finished the soles of shoes. The newspaper reported that Swain had made significant improvements to the sanded lathe and that, with his two sons, he had finished the soles of 5,250 pairs of shoes in one year. Another small factory, owned by A.D. Towle from Lynn, Massachusetts, opened on Center Street to make "ladies boots and shoes."

In 1860, Gardner Kingman of Bridgewater, Massachusetts, opened another shoe factory. Kingman was still in business in 1862 in the midst of the Civil War. The newspaper reported that the war's demand for shoes and boots made the company's prospects "very cheering." However, the factory did not last through the war.

Simeon Lewis opened another shoe factory after the Civil War. Lewis went to Bridgewater to learn the shoemaking business. His factory was still in business three years later, but how long the small company stayed in business is unclear, as it disappears from the records.

When the town sold the West School House on Howard Street in 1871, the building was converted into Mitchell and Hayden's Shoe Factory. A reporter wrote about watching "mysteries of shoe making by steam," and young ladies stitching and pasting under the watchful direction of a supervisor. Mitchell and Hayden's factory operated until 1873, when it burned down.

Despite the number of times that shoe manufacturing was tried on the island, it was only moderately successful and never employed enough people to make a major difference in Nantucket's economy.

A linen coat factory, owned by John W. Hallett, opened in 1878 and employed one hundred people; that year, fifteen thousand coats were turned out on seventy-five machines. But it, too, was short-lived.

One endeavor that did make a significant contribution for a while was the Atlantic Straw Factory that opened in the 1850s and did not close until 1866.

The first mention of the straw company appeared in 1853 when the *Inquirer* reported that Justin Lawrence was investing money in a business that "would give profitable employment to an immense number of females." A building was bought and refurbished at 76 Main Street, a building that had previously been a Quaker meetinghouse. Despite recognizing the need for a new source of income, Nantucketers worried that the straw factory might become a sweatshop in their midst. Spokesmen for the company tried to allay their fears, assuring the town that the factory would not be "servile" in nature and that bells would not be rung to announce work hours.

Within several months, the straw factory employed over two hundred women "making very handsome wages." It occasionally opened its doors to visitors, and the year after it opened, over one thousand people visited in just one month. Several years later, a reporter wrote that each young woman sat on a revolving "cushioned chair" that could be raised or lowered and that there were "no task masters, no grouty overseers, no sunrise bell."

The company made the straw hats then in vogue. Straw was braided, and molds were used to shape a variety of hats for men, women and children. In 1855, the factory produced a good number of hats: 9,000 women's bonnets and 138,000 men's hats. The newspaper reported that the factory distributed "tens of thousands of dollars" in much-needed wages.

The straw factory had a complicated history with multiple changes of ownership and intermittent closures, some lasting for months. In 1858, for example, the factory was closed, and the parent company in Foxboro collected its chairs and tables. "Eleven young ladies" from the island went to Foxboro to continue working for the company.

Within several months, however, the company reopened its Nantucket branch. Remarkably, it sent a woman, Miss Mowry, to oversee the operation. But within months, the factory closed again, to reopen during the winter of 1859. During the Civil War, workers bought material and donated their time to make a large flag that was raised over the customhouse with much patriotic fanfare. The *Inquirer* exclaimed, "Hurrah for the girls!"

The factory stayed open for only a short time after the war. At the end of 1865, it advertised "fancy skating caps and children's turbans" as Christmas presents. But it was a losing proposition to maintain the factory, so when

Atlantic Hall, circa 1860. On its original site at 74 Main Street, it served as a Quaker meetinghouse, straw factory, assembly hall and an indoor cycling and roller-skating rink. It was moved to Brant Point in the 1880s to become part of the Nantucket Hotel and was floated back across the harbor in 1904 to its present resting point on South Water Street, where it is part of the Dreamland Theater. *Nantucket Historical Association.*

the building closed its doors the next time, they stayed closed. The building was put up for auction in October 1866, and within a month, it was sold and renamed Atlantic Hall. The new owners redesigned the second floor to accommodate dances, concerts and lectures. It became Nantucket's largest assembly hall and a part-time bicycle rink and roller-skating rink.

While the straw factory never returned to Atlantic Hall, it did manage to revive one more time. Miss Mowry advertised for fifty straw workers almost six years later in 1872. But it was a short-lived venture, and straw making left Nantucket for good.

Nevertheless, making straw hats was Nantucket's most successful factory in the post-whaling era. Factories simply were not suited to the island's location. Luckily, it was not long afterward that the next "industry" began to emerge, one that would save Nantucket's economy: tourism.

In fact, the building that made the transition from a Quaker meetinghouse to a factory to an assembly hall and sports rink epitomizes the economic progress of the island up to the present.

In the mid-1880s, Atlantic Hall was sold to a developer from Boston who bought land in Brant Point. Atlantic Hall was moved to Brant Point, where it became the center of the grand Nantucket Hotel complex that opened for the 1884 summer season. The luxury hotel operated until 1904, when it was sold at public auction to a men's fraternity, the Improved Order of Red Men. The building was floated across the harbor to its latest resting point on South Water Street, where it sits today.

The Red Men used the upper floor for their meetings and rented out the downstairs. In 1907, the town held its annual town meeting there. The same year, Nantucket's first motion picture was shown downstairs at Smith and Blanchard's Moving Picture Show. In 1911, four men formed the Dreamland Theater Company and showed the island's first talking picture in 1930. The Dreamland was purchased in 2006 by the Dreamland Foundation and extensively renovated. It opened its doors in 2012 as a community arts center and movie theater. You can't help but wonder what the Quakers would have made of the many permutations of their meetinghouse.

7

Grogshops within Our Borders!

Nantucketers waged a variety of moral crusades against "King Alcohol" throughout the 1800s. The century saw the rise and fall of temperance groups that each pressured the town to eliminate the sale of alcohol. Those Nantucketers would be appalled at the prevalence of alcohol in Nantucket now with its many trendy bars and its liquor and wine stores.

Nantucket's port was typical of a working port of the era. The neighborhood around our wharves had seedy saloons called grogshops, as well as a number of brothels. As early as 1817, town fathers expressed concern about people who wasted their "meager earnings" on drink. And while

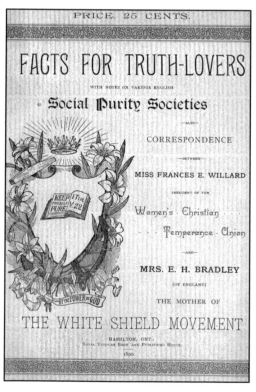

A pamphlet from the Women's Christian Temperance Union. *Nantucket Historical Association.*

they were frequented mostly by sailors, the *Inquirer* reported that "no class was excluded" from the "haunts of debauchery."

In 1822, the town established the Quaise Asylum, intended as a poorhouse and farm as well as a place for drunkards to become sober.

The first temperance society on the island was organized in 1832 after a visit by John Marsh, leader of the national American Temperance Union. Marsh's two-hour lecture about the evils of alcohol struck a chord with islanders. Shortly thereafter, public meetings were held to discuss what to do about the problem, including one at the Methodist church attended by over one thousand people. The all-male Nantucket Association for the Promotion of Temperance was organized in October 1832 with four hundred members. William Mitchell, astronomer, educator and father of the famous astronomer Maria Mitchell, was elected president.

The association targeted alcohol use by all but focused especially on visiting mariners. Congregational pastor Stephen Mason noted, "Nantucket is notoriously the place from which inebriates of other places on all the neighboring coast receive their supplies of poison when unable to procure it in their own vicinity." The association tried to enlist local merchants and ship owners to encourage sobriety on board whaling ships. They met with some success. In 1833, the association reported that eleven of seventeen ships had sailed from the island without "ardent spirits" on board, with the exception of small quantities reserved "for medicinal purposes." It also reported that several retailers of grogshops had relinquished their businesses and that twenty-four "common drunkards" had been sent to the Quaise Asylum, their intemperance blamed on "rum drinking on the oceans."

In 1838, a Seaman's Society was organized to encourage sailors to give up alcohol. For one, drunken sailors were a hazard on board. The Seaman's Society encouraged "dry" boardinghouses for sailors waiting for berths on ships. One such boardinghouse, owned by Jarvis Robinson, was on Washington Street.

In the 1840s, a clause was added to the shipping papers of many vessels leaving Nantucket: "No distilled spirituous liquors will be put on board this vessel by the Owner, except for strictly medicinal use." Sailors on those ships had to swear to abstain from liquor on board during the entire voyage; a sailor caught in violation could forfeit his entire salary, a severe penalty indeed as whaling ships embarked on multi-year expeditions.

Places of "infamy and death," however, continued to proliferate. Two new temperance societies were organized in 1834: the Young Men's Total

THE PLEDGE.

Nantucket, June 18, 1844.

OUR PRINCIPLES, "TEMPERANCE".——OUR WEAPON, "MORAL SUASION."

THE PLEDGE

IS PUBLISHED AT WASHINGTON HALL.

TERMS—6 1-4 cents per copy.

INQUIRER PRESS.

To THE PUBLIC. Two years ago, when the last Temperance Fair was held, it was thought that a paper would add to the attraction, and also be a pecuniary advantage, and accordingly the experiment was tried. The result was eminently successful, the treasury being swelled, and it is to be hoped that the readers derived some useful instruction from the perusal. Believing that an effort of the same character, would be patronised with an equal degree of liberality this year, and also that it would tend in some degree to increase the interest in the cause of Temperance, we have thought it would not seem

"I'll tell it you, as 'twas told me."

At a Temperance Meeting, convened in one of our seaport towns, a gentleman arose, and avowed himself a Temperance Advocate, and stated that he wished to relate a story, himself being the voucher for its correctness.— Permission being granted, he gave as follows:—"In a southern city, a few years since, an unusual bustle was observed in a hitherto quiet street in the upper part of the city. On inquiring the cause, it was ascertained that the accomplished Caroline Montague was that evening to be united in marriage to William Hastings, a young gentleman of high intellectual as well as moral attainments. Caroline was the only child of a wealthy Quaker in the city,

dared surmise. He was in the full tide of success in his profession, and yet his eye had lost its wonted brightness, and his step its elasticity. Their former acquaintances they ceased to visit, without giving any well defined reason, and it was at this juncture, that Caroline was seized with an alarming illness, which terminated her existence in a few short days. The friends who saw her during her sickness, were surprised at her appearance, but they forbore to probe the feelings of her relatives by irrelevant questions.— She died and was followed to the grave by multitudes who had known her in brighter hours, but a mystery seemed to hang over every thing connected with her. But the fearful truth at length came out. Caroline loved the pleasures of the exhilerating cup.

Nantucket temperance newspaper. *Nantucket Atheneum.*

Abstinence Society and the Colored Temperance Society. The latter elected ex–whaling captain Edward J. Pompey as president.

Reformers sought to limit the number of liquor licenses permitted on the island. Limiting licenses, however, drove the trade underground. In 1836, for example, the town licensed only one establishment to dispense alcohol and it only for medicinal purposes. It also noted that illegal grogshops could easily be found, most operating out of rooms in private houses or in boardinghouses. In addition, legitimate businesses often sold liquor under the counter.

Periodically, the town cracked down on the businesses that flouted the laws. In 1836, Jonathan Hall was indicted for selling liquor and fined twenty dollars. Robert F. Parker announced in the newspaper that he had been forced to shut down his alcohol trade but took a swipe at temperance leaders, who, he claimed, "all at some times" required his "articles." Shortly thereafter, he brazenly advertised that he, once again, had liquor for sale in his Town's Notion Store, advertising that, for "the intemperate community," he had "a few extra *notions* of superior quality."

Businessmen also used their public stance against alcohol to encourage business. For example, when William Robinson opened a barbershop in the mid-1830s, he announced that his shop would adhere to the "strictest rules of temperance" and shun "spirituous liquors as sedulously as a lamb would flee from the presence of a tiger."

The most popular temperance group of the 1840s was the Washingtonian Total Abstinence Society. Started in Maryland by six reformed alcoholics, this organization focused more on individual reform than on legislation, rather like Alcoholics Anonymous today. As such, it renounced politics and discouraged discussion of other topics, such as abolition, at its meetings. The Nantucket chapter rented a room on the second floor of a building on Main Street named Temperance Hall, where it met and kept a reading room open to the public.

The Washingtonians ushered in a movement that remained popular long after the demise of their organization—public renunciation of alcohol, also known as "taking the pledge." In the first few weeks of 1841, the newspaper reported that more than five hundred islanders had vowed in front of their friends and neighbors to remain abstinent.

The Nantucket chapter issued its own newspaper, the *Bill of Fare*, for a brief time in 1842. In one of its two issues, the paper offered $1,000 to "anyone who will write an essay proving clearly that ardent spirits are good for our physical constitution." The paper closed before the reward could be given.

A major accomplishment of the Washingtonians was the transformation of the barroom of the Nantucket Hotel, now the Dreamland Theater, into a temperance gathering spot. Their fervor also prompted Timothy Calder to put an ad in the newspaper to quell the rumor that he kept "ardent spirits" in his store, noting his membership in the organization.

The Washingtonian Society was one of the most successful temperance organizations on Nantucket. A letter to the editor may have exaggerated its success in reforming alcoholics, writing that a "few years since there were hundreds of miserable drunkards in our streets—*literally* in our streets. There were then in Nantucket over 300 drunkards and *drunkardesses* AND 286 OF THESE miserable inebriates—256 men and 30 women—have been snatched, as brands from the burning, from the reeking haunts of intemperance."

One of the most fascinating temperance groups to be spun off the Washingtonians was the Cold Water Army. Started on the island in 1841, the Cold Water Army was made up of children who pledged never to start drinking alcohol. At its height, the Cold Water Army astonishingly comprised over seven hundred youngsters. The *Bill of Fare* reported that the seven hundred marched in "gallant style" to the annual Fourth of July celebration of 1842. The following week, a letter praised the youngsters for enlivening what was generally "a dull day at Nantucket. We are a quiet people." The writer said the parade was "a beautiful sight" led by their "commander in chief," Dr. Charles F. Winslow.

Before 1850, women participated in their own temperance auxiliaries. They sponsored local fairs to raise money and awareness for the cause. Admission to one such fair in 1842 charged twelve and a half cents for general admission and six cents to members of the Cold Water Army. The women were not reluctant to take action; in 1843, they reported that several members had bravely visited the homes of "loathsome dens of intemperance" and "transformed them into pleasant homes." A letter praised the women for leaving "their comfortable firesides to carry light and joy into the chilling haunts of intemperance."

On occasion, the various temperance groups came together for lectures and dinners. At one such dinner, they toasted to their "War on King Alcohol" and to "pure water, the most wholesome beverage that we possess."

Law enforcement was stepped up because of pressure from the Washingtonians. Several grogshops were closed and purveyors of illegal alcohol prosecuted. Eunice Folger, for example, was charged as "a common drunkard" and sentenced to the House of Correction for six months.

Intriguingly, the temperance leaders did not wage war against opium, as its use was not seen as a problem. In 1845, J.F. Macy's store advertised the receipt of "a further supply of the Elixir of Opium."

In the mid-1840s, temperance on the island was reorganized; by then, the Washingtonians had fallen victim to sectarian politics, and membership had fallen off. The Nantucket Total Abstinence Society, or Sons of Temperance, replaced it in 1846. The society met at Temperance, or Harmony, Hall on the site of St. Mary's Catholic Church. The Cold Water Army continued under its leadership.

But by the end of the 1840s, the temperance movement had lost its appeal, and membership dwindled to a few of the faithful. As a result, liquor sales crept up. The *Inquirer* noted that "quite a number of reformed men have relapsed into their old habits." The Sons of Temperance reported that there were eleven places that sold liquor "by the glass" and that there were also numerous rented rooms used as grogshops. The newspaper reported a rowdy and drunken night on Fair Street. The adverse publicity had an effect, and the temperance movement gained steam again. High school principal Augustus Morse addressed town officials concerned about the "lotteries, gambling houses, rum shops and beer shops…at the corners of our streets!"

Temperance gained ground during the 1850s, even though the population of the island had plummeted due to the demise of whaling, the Great Fire of 1846 and the California Gold Rush. The first-ever liquor seizure took place just before Christmas 1852. The sheriff and his deputies conducted a simultaneous raid in several island neighborhoods on four suppliers of alcohol. These were the shops of Elizabeth Griffiths in Gunner Alley, Michael Nevins of Hussey Street, Abraham Pease of Federal Street and William Mullen of Rose Lane. Seven or eight barrels, a keg and about fifteen jugs of liquor were seized and destroyed at three of the establishments. No liquor was found at Mullen's; the temperance committee claimed that his customers had received a tip and taken it away before the raid.

No rum seller received more than a twenty-dollar fine. Within a year, "rum holes" were reported to have actually *increased* on the island since the raid. One letter accused rum sellers of murder. "There are no less than twenty of those dens of iniquity in this village." As a result, "two of our citizens have died very suddenly from intoxication; they were generous, noble hearted men, devoted to their families when sober. They were literally murdered for rum was given them freely." The writer placed blame on town officials who looked the other way, as well as on the Irish community, indicative of the anti-Irish sentiment rampant in the United States at the time.

Less than a month later, the newspaper reported two separate incidents of intoxication that almost resulted in more loss of life. On two freezing evenings in January, the night watchman picked up a drunken man and a drunken woman who would have frozen to death had he not come along and carried them to their homes.

Temperance took a back seat during and after the Civil War but enjoyed a revival in the mid-1870s. The *Inquirer and Mirror* reported that temperance had begun "to make itself manifest" again with the formation of the Nantucket Union of Temperance, led by a group of "war horses," elderly people who had been active in previous temperance organizations. In fact, temperance became the dominant reform movement of the decade. The crusade to "take the pledge" became so popular that the town hall was hardly "large enough to hold the crowds," and within a few months, over 350 Nantucketers had publicly declared their total abstinence. The next year, over 500 Nantucketers petitioned the state legislature to pass stringent anti-alcohol laws. This was a huge number of people because the population of the island had dipped to just over 4,000 people.

A "Temperance Club-Room" opened at the Lodge Building on Main Street for "gentlemen accustomed to spend their evenings and spare time in the drinking saloon." Within a month, the room, which had been outfitted with games and an organ, was a great success, with seventy-one men having "affixed their names to the pledge in the room." This time, the organization was fully integrated and included men from the black community.

Throughout the 1870s, the group sponsored multiple lectures and open-air temperance rallies, usually at the top of Main Street in front of the Pacific Bank. Speakers included Nantucket-born William F. Barnard, superintendent of the Five Points House of Industry in New York City and, in his retirement, the first president of the Nantucket Historical Association. Barnard spoke about what he had seen of the "ravages" of alcohol in the slums of New York City.

"No license" was the battle cry as temperance societies lobbied to eliminate all liquor licensing in Massachusetts. Despite their valiant efforts, they were not successful. In 1877, the legislature narrowly defeated a prohibition law. A month later, Nantucket's temperance leaders failed to convince the selectmen to eliminate all liquor licenses on the island, and in 1881, the town rejected another anti-licensing motion. Another major push to make Nantucket a dry community occurred in 1887 with temperance leaders accusing the selectmen of being in league with the "liquor men and saloonists." As before, the efforts to stamp out the sale of alcohol failed.

The selectmen were understandably reluctant to make Nantucket a dry community. The island economy was slowly reviving due to the growing summer tourist trade. The selectmen

A pamphlet from the Woman's Christian Temperance Union. *Nantucket Historical Association.*

began to issue liquor licenses to hotels like the Springfield House on South Water Street, catering to summer visitors.

A chapter of the powerful Woman's Christian Temperance Union (WCTU) was established on the island in 1880. The local chapter was active and supported by leaders from the black and white communities. Members wore white ribbons to show their support of temperance. The growing women's suffrage movement also backed temperance.

There were periodic crackdowns on liquor establishments, often in response to complaints of the temperance societies. In 1884, Charles M. Thomas and Charles C. Thomas were arraigned for "maintaining a liquor nuisance and for illegally keeping a pool table." Although they were found guilty, their fines were minor.

In 1891, however, the "no license" movement finally achieved victory when the town voted to eliminate all liquor licenses. At long last, after decades of agitation, Nantucket was dry, the sale of alcohol not even permitted for medicinal purposes. But after several "dry" months, even two ministers urged the selectmen to grant a license to "some responsible person for the sale of liquor for medicinal use," although the WCTU vehemently opposed the request. By that summer, the selectmen had

Two men outside a store on Straight Wharf, circa 1895. *Nantucket Historical Association.*

granted Richard E. Congdon the sole license to dispense liquor "for mechanical and medicinal purposes."

Nantucket's initial experiment with prohibition lasted two more years, after which the selectmen granted three more licenses, and the door to legal alcohol was opened, not to be closed until the next big temperance movement in the early 1900s that culminated in Prohibition.

8

"Exhilarating Exercise"

People who come to Nantucket today have many sports from which to pick. Entire clubs are devoted to some of them, often involving expensive and exclusive memberships. You can play golf, disc golf, tennis, handball, squash and paddle tennis, among others. And although known for summer sports, Nantucketers have long enjoyed winter activities such as sledding, ice skating and ice fishing. It has been possible to ice skate year round since

Baseball game around 1910 with houses on the Cliff in the background. *Nantucket Historical Association.*

View looking north overlooking Jetties Beach with a sailboat race in the distance, circa 1930. *Nantucket Historical Association.*

2002 with the building of the Nantucket Ice Community Rink. Watersports attract many summer visitors. Activities on, or in, the water include fishing, sailing, kayaking, surfing, water skiing, stand-up paddle boarding, kite sailing, beach volleyball and swimming. The island boasts two yacht clubs, a country club and four golf courses. An extensive system of bicycle paths is used by those who bike often and by those who bike only on vacation. Running is also a popular activity.

Many yearly events are scheduled around sports. Among them are two premier sailing races, the Figawi Race and the Opera House Cup Race for classic wooden sailboats. The island hosts a variety of marathons, triathlons, fishing and golf tournaments and bike races.

It was not always so. For much of our history, people did not come to Nantucket to play. They came to work.

The Puritans of the Massachusetts Bay Colony did not encourage frivolity or wasting time; they especially disapproved of any activity that might involve gambling. However, they did approve of, and encourage, physical health and fitness. Daily life required a lot of physical labor, and most people did not need to add anything to their lives to keep fit. This is not to say that early New Englanders did not participate in some form of sport. Humans naturally compete, and the Puritans were not immune to that instinct. Simple contests such as who could run across a field the fastest, throw a rock the farthest, hit a target, ride the fastest horse or catch the biggest fish were part of everyday life.

Activities involving balls and sticks go back centuries, and games involving bats and balls were popular during the Revolutionary War. Most of those early sports were unstructured and often rough-and-tumble with few recognized rules.

After the Civil War, sports in the United States proliferated and became organized. As today, some required expensive gear and were the domain of the well-to-do, while others were more egalitarian. As Nantucket began to cater to the tourist trade, it is not surprising that the island promoted several sports to attract off-island visitors.

One such sport was bicycling. Just after the Civil War, early bicycles, known as velocipedes, came to the island. These were nothing like the sleek and smooth-riding bicycles of today. The first mass-produced velocipedes were "bone shakers," made of wood with metal tires. The fad of riding them swept the nation in the 1860s and 1870s; indoor rinks opened where people could rent and ride velocipedes. In 1869, Atlantic Hall, now the Dreamland Theater, was converted to accommodate velocipedes. The *Inquirer and Mirror* noted that the hall was "daily and nightly filled with young men anxiously waiting their turn for a ride on the firey [*sic*] steed."

As bicycles evolved, more people purchased their own to ride outdoors. J. Stockley Cary brought a bike to the island in 1886; it had a large front wheel and a small back one. It did not take long before races were organized to see who could ride the fastest.

The "golden age" of bicycles was from the late 1880s through the turn of the century. Cycling's popularity went hand in hand with bicycle improvement as bicycles began to look like the familiar bike of today. The new bikes were safer, with chain drives and equally sized tires. These bicycles were more accessible to new riders, including women. The League of American Wheelmen promoted bicycle safety, the rights of cyclists and the paving of roads. Members of Nantucket's earliest bicycle club, the Weweeder Cycling Club, were members of the Wheelmen.

A quarter-mile bike-racing track was built on Lower Orange Street in 1895 by Eugene S. Burgess in the vicinity of today's Marine Lumber. The following year, Nantucket built its first bicycle path. The unpaved path went from town to 'Sconset. Two years later, a second bicycle path was built from the waterworks by Washing Pond to Madaket, not far from the water storage tank on Cliff Road today. The *Inquirer and Mirror* reported in 1898 that Edward Morey had cycled from 'Sconset to town in a record-breaking time of eighteen and a half minutes. In the early 1900s, another bicycle path was built to Wauwinet along the Polpis Road.

The popularity of bicycling waned with the arrival of automobiles, and no new bicycle paths were built on the island until after World War II. The

Weweeder Cycling Club at Monument Square, circa 1890. *Nantucket Historical Association.*

challenge now is to find a safe route for bicycles in town, especially during the busy summer months.

Swimming began to be popular around the same time as cycling. It is amazing to consider that many sailors did not know how to swim and drowned at sea. When the sport of swimming became popular, it is not surprising that Nantucket began to promote its beaches as a way to attract tourism. In 1875, Captain Matthew Webb became a celebrity as the first man to swim the English Channel, and his fame helped promote the sport. (His feat was not replicated for over thirty-six years.) In 1882, Webb visited Nantucket and gave a well-attended swimming exhibition at Surfside Beach.

Like cycling, swimming was promoted as a sport accessible to women. The *Inquirer and Mirror* advised girls in 1870, "It is quite time you began to swim," promoting swimming as a "powerful and hygienic agent" and "exhilarating exercise."

The beaches of Coatue were advertised as a vacation spot, especially wonderful for swimming. The Coatue Land Company laid out 141 plots of land in the mid-1880s, including sites for a clubhouse, a pier, a hotel, stores

Cedar Beach House and pier on Coatue, circa 1886. *Nantucket Historical Association.*

and cottages. The company hoped to provide daily ferry service from town to the narrow barrier peninsula that encloses Nantucket's harbor. A few lots were sold, and a few cottages and a grocery store were built. Optimistic reports speculated that there would eventually be enough people to warrant the addition of a post office! In addition, a bathing pavilion, complete with a "toboggan water slide," was built. The slide was in use for five years; an advertisement promised to provide visitors with "suits, bathrooms, toboggans and swings." In 1890, H.G. Worth built a gun house for those who wanted to go trap shooting, and in 1893, there was an unfounded rumor that the New York Yacht Club was contemplating building a clubhouse on Coatue. However, the building scheme eventually failed, and daily ferry service never materialized. More schemes to develop Coatue were proposed as late as 1898, when the peninsula was resurveyed. Today, there are still privately owned land and cottages on Coatue, but most of the fragile area is protected under the auspices of the Coskata-Coatue Wildlife Refuge and accessible only by private watercraft or four-wheel drive vehicles with special permits.

At a special town meeting in 1904, the town voted unanimously to lease what is now known as "Jetties Beach" to Clifford Folger. Although Folger had moved to Framingham, he reminded the voters of his Nantucket roots and assured them he was neither a speculator nor an investor. He said he did not "like the idea of the control of the beach passing into the hands of

Cliff Bathing Beach, now Jetties Beach, circa 1920. *Nantucket Historical Association.*

parties who were not Nantucketers or interested in Nantucket" and feared the beach "might be conducted in an objectionable manner and made into a class of resort which the people of Nantucket did not want on the island." The town gave him a fifteen-year lease for $350 a year for what was then called the "Cliff Bathing Beach."

That first summer, Folger built a multipurpose pavilion where food was served and that had separate wings for men's and women's bathrooms, as well as several rows of bathhouses in which to change. That building is still in use today. It was not until 1937 that the area started to be called "the Jetties" after the jetties that form the entrance to Nantucket Harbor. (The jetties were built between 1880 and 1911 and are due to be refurbished in 2015.)

In 1906, an enclosed heated saltwater pool with bathhouses was opened at the beach in 'Sconset to cater to the increasingly popular summer community. The pool was used for just over ten years, ceasing operations in 1917. The pool was moved across the street and used as the foundation for a cottage in Codfish Park known as The Buoy.

Tennis was another popular sport in the late nineteenth century. The first U.S. Open was played in Newport, Rhode Island, in 1881. Nantucket's first tennis courts were at private clubs. The first report of a tennis tournament was in 1897 at the Springfield House, a hotel on North Water Street. The match was won by "Mr. Echeverria." When the 'Sconset Casino opened in 1900, it had two clay tennis courts; five more were added by 1909.

The *Inquirer and Mirror* reported in 1907 that tennis was quickly becoming one of the island's most popular pastimes. That was the year that the

A mixed doubles tennis match between 'Sconset and the Yacht Club, circa 1907. *Nantucket Historical Association.*

Nantucket Athletic Club constructed its first tennis courts. Three clay courts were built at the corner of Broad and Beach Streets where the Nantucket Yacht Club is today. In the summers, weekly tournaments between the Casino and the Athletic Club were "largely attended and decidedly interesting." The fiercely contested matches took all day as the participants and spectators traveled back and forth by horse and buggy. The host club was responsible for serving lunch.

Tennis can be played today at many venues, most of them private. These include eleven courts at the 'Sconset Casino and twelve courts at the Nantucket Yacht Club. The Westmoor Country Club has thirteen courts, and there are four courts at Sankaty Golf Club. The only town-owned courts are the six at Jetties Beach.

Summer visitors were also responsible for creating Nantucket's golf courses. All golf courses on the island are links style and follow the natural contours of the land. Two courses lay claim to being the first golf course on the island, but most sources agree that it was the Nantucket Golf Course on the north shore along Cliff Road that was the first. That course came about because summer visitor David Noyes told his friend Sidney Chase in 1897 that he no longer planned to spend his summers on Nantucket because there were no golf courses. That summer, Chase and two other summer residents laid out a course near the waterworks. Their project was immediately successful; about one hundred people signed up as members.

The clubhouse of the Nantucket Golf Club on Cliff Road. The club opened in 1897. The building is now the headquarters of the Nantucket Conservation Foundation. *Nantucket Historical Association.*

At first a tent served as their clubhouse, but in 1899, a permanent clubhouse was built. Sheep and goats were used to maintain the nine-hole course, which eventually expanded to eighteen holes. Pauline Mackay, the women's champion of the United States in 1905, played there in the early days of her career.

Although that golf course no longer exists, remnants can be seen now at Tupancy Links, a seventy-three-acre property owned by the Nantucket Conservation Foundation. Between 1976 and 1987, Sallie Harris and Oswald Tupancy donated the land, which has become one of Nantucket's most popular and beautiful walking areas with trails leading to a bluff looking over the harbor. The golf course's clubhouse is used as administrative offices by the foundation.

Less than a year after Nantucket Golf Club opened, the Siasconset Golf Course was begun, although some sources claim golf had been played there since 1894. Either way, the course was short-lived and had disappeared by the 1920s.

The oldest golf course still in use on Nantucket, the Siasconset Golf Club, was laid out in 1899. It is considered the oldest privately owned golf course in the United States that is open to the public, although its ownership recently passed from private hands. For most of its history, the Siasconset course had nine holes, although for a brief time between the world wars,

Sankaty Head Golf Course, 2014. *Mark White.*

there were eighteen holes. And in its early days, the greens were square! Today, the course is affectionately known by the locals as "Skinner's," named after Robert "Skinner" Coffin, who was its superintendent for many years. Remarkably, the clubhouse, built before the turn of the century, is still in use. The Nantucket Land Bank and the Sconset Trust bought the property in 2012 to prevent it from being developed, and the company that manages Miacomet Golf Course now manages Skinner's.

The next golf course built on Nantucket was Sankaty Head Golf Course. Considered a premier links course, it has changed little since it was opened in the early 1920s. Sankaty, with its commanding views of Sankaty Lighthouse, was built largely due to the efforts of multimillionaire David Gray, who donated 280 acres and a beautiful clubhouse for its original one hundred members.

Sankaty has one of the few remaining caddie camps in the United States, where approximately sixty boys have come every summer since it opened during the Great Depression. The mess hall and one of the dorms were destroyed in a propane fire during the summer of 2011, but money was quickly raised to rebuild the facilities.

It was not until 1963 that year-round Nantucketers got a public golf course to call their own when Ralph Marble turned his dairy farm into a golf course. In the mid-1980s, the Nantucket Land Bank bought the Miacomet course to protect it from development. In 2003, the course was expanded to eighteen holes, and the original nine holes were extensively refurbished in 2008.

The most recent golf course on the island is the exclusive, members-only Nantucket Golf Club, with membership fees among the highest in the

View of the roller-skating rink, circa 1880, located at the site of the present Yacht Club. *Nantucket Historical Association.*

world, reported to be over $300,000. Built in 1997 on the Milestone Road, it is considered a world-class course. Part of the course was created when the heirs of Skinner Coffin sold 250 acres of land to the new club for over $8 million. The closest tourists and most islanders will get to the course is along the bicycle path to 'Sconset.

Another sport enthusiastically embraced by Nantucket during the era when sports began to flourish was roller skating. Skate design benefited from the evolution of bicycles as skates incorporated axles and ball bearings. The first mass-produced roller skates in the United States appeared in the 1880s. Early skaters were confined to indoor rinks. Nantucket Roller Skating Rink opened in 1880 in Atlantic Hall, now the Dreamland Theater. The hall was on Main Street at the time. An early advertisement boasted that skaters would enjoy the music of the Skating Rink Orchestra while skating on the hall's new surface. The management promised that "gentlemanly attendants" would be on hand to assist beginners and that the rink would be "conducted in a manner that will meet the approbation of the most fastidious." An advertisement noted that skating had become "a fashionable pastime...particularly healthful...indulged in extensively by the best classes." It cost a dime to rent skates and fifteen to twenty-five cents to skate in the afternoon or evenings.

Nationally known skater Miss Jessie LaFone, promoted as the "Prima Donna of Skates," gave several exhibitions during the week of the

Ice skating around the steamship *Island Home*, stuck in the ice in 1893. *Nantucket Historical Association.*

"Grand Opening" of the summer season in June 1885. An off-island band accompanied the skaters that summer. The rink was closed when the hall was sold and moved to Brant Point, where it formed the core of a hotel.

Although there had been a bowling alley on Nantucket as early as 1833 on the site where the Dreamland Theater now is, as well as a bowling alley in 'Sconset, bowling did not become widespread until the 1880s, when the bowling craze swept Nantucket. Alleys featured duckpins, which local boys were hired to reset.

In 1887, there was an ad for a bowling alley with four lanes and a billiard parlor for sale on South Water Street that had apparently shut down. Another bowling alley opened in August 1891 at the Surfside Hotel that catered to the summer visitors who arrived there by train from the steamship terminal.

The bowling craze also hit 'Sconset, and the casino built two bowling alleys in an annex in 1909 that continued to operate until 1920, when the building was sold.

However, the Nantucket Athletic Club on the site of the Nantucket Yacht Club built the most successful bowling alley of the era. While the club's tennis courts and yachting facilities were frequented by summer visitors, bowling attracted a local crowd in the off-season. Tournaments were reported in detail every week in the newspaper. A sample: "Wednesday evening it was the battle of the butchers, and when Bennett was through rolling he had shrunk up like a sausage."

Candlepin bowling lanes at the Mid-Island Bowl owned by Roger Young, circa 1964. *Nantucket Historical Association.*

Bowling season culminated in an annual tournament every May against archrival Brockton, Massachusetts, and the towns hosted the several-day affair on alternating years. For example, forty-four islanders traveled to Brockton in 1913 to bowl or to cheer on the local teams. Although the Nantucketers lost that year, the trip gave the islanders the chance to travel in automobiles that were then "barred from the confines of the island."

For several years, students at the Academy Hill School walked down the hill to the Athletic Club to use its facilities for physical education, including the use of the bowling alleys.

From 1943 through 1949, Preston Manchester operated Nantucket Bowling Alley on Main Street where the restaurant Met on Main is now. And Roger Young operated Mid-Island Bowl with eight candlepin alleys from 1964 to 1983. Harvey Young, the present owner of Young's Bicycles, reported that, when he was a child, he thought that the alley was built just for him by his father. Unfortunately, there are no places to bowl on the island today; islanders take their children to bowl on the Cape.

While the island may have the reputation for being the playground of the wealthy with expensive and exclusive clubs, there are still many sports that Nantucketers and visitors can enjoy with little to no investment.

9

Nantucket's Love Affair with Coffee

N antucket has had a long love affair with coffee. Today, coffee is found in many places, and coffee shops are popular gathering spots. But Nantucket's love affair with coffee began long ago.

Coffee became a popular drink in the American colonies as a protest against the British tax on tea, and stores on Nantucket have stocked coffee since that time. Coffee became an important trading item for Nantucket merchants as its popularity grew. According to ships' logs at the Nantucket Historical Association, coffee was a staple drink on board whaling ships; for example, in 1799, the Nantucket ship *Criterion* went to Java "chiefly for coffee." And in 1855, the crew of the whaler *Potomac* complained that they had gone three long days without coffee or tea.

Nantucket names have become synonymous with coffee. Who has not heard of Folgers or Starbucks Coffee? Folgers Coffee, one of the world's largest coffee producers, has its roots on Nantucket. But Starbucks, found on street corners around the world, actually does *not* have a Nantucket connection, and there is no Starbucks Coffee on Nantucket. The Starbucks founders took the name from Melville's *Moby Dick*, which does have a connection with the island. (Melville, who did not visit the island until after the publication of *Moby Dick*, based the book on the harrowing tale of the *Essex*, recently popularized by Nathaniel Philbrick's book *In the Heart of the Sea: The Tragedy of the Whaleship Essex* and a movie of the same name.)

The Folger family landed on the island in 1659 when Peter Folger was hired to do some surveying for the original proprietors. One of the few white settlers to learn the Wampanoag language, he promoted peaceable relations between the Indians and the settlers.

Generations of Folgers lived on the island in all manner of occupations, some who prospered and some who did not. A good many left the island to seek riches and a better life elsewhere. Perhaps Peter Folger's most famous descendant is his grandson Benjamin Franklin, the eighth child of his daughter Abiah Folger, who left the island when she married Josiah Franklin. Benjamin Franklin frequented coffeehouses when he lived in London because they were meeting places for the intellectuals and liberals of the day.

James A. Folger, founder of Folgers Coffee Company. *Nantucket Historical Association.*

The Great Fire of 1846 burned one-third of Nantucket's buildings and devastated the economy. It consumed the island's business infrastructure, much of it built around whaling. Three of the four wharves, whale oil warehouses, ropewalks and a variety of shops went up in flames. More than eight hundred people were made homeless overnight. Nantucket's whaling industry never fully recovered from the blow, and it was not long before New Bedford surpassed the island in whaling, partly due to the fire but also because of New Bedford's access to the railroads. The final blow was when petroleum replaced whale oil.

After the Great Fire, it was hard for Nantucketers to find jobs, and when gold was discovered in California in 1849, young men left the island in droves. Idle Nantucket whale ships transported many of the forty-niners to the West Coast, most never to return. Timber from those ships was used to construct buildings in San Francisco.

Samuel B. Folger was among those ruined by the Great Fire. His tryworks that converted whale blubber into oil was destroyed, as were his two whale ships that were unfortunately tied up at the docks that fateful night. In 1849, the family pooled their meager resources to fund the voyage of three sons to seek fame and fortune in the gold fields of California. Edward, age twenty; Henry, age sixteen; and James, age fourteen, boarded a ship to Panama. The brothers undertook the dangerous crossing of the isthmus, traveling by boat up the Chagres River and hiking fifteen miles through the jungle. Like many of the forty-niners, they waited for weeks to get berths on a steamer headed for California. They finally arrived in San Francisco in the spring of 1850.

Mining supplies and transportation to the gold fields were expensive, and the brothers decided to use the family's savings to pay for Edward and Henry to look for gold and leave the youngest, James, behind to find steady work. Despite the influx of so many young men, it was easy to find a job in San Francisco. Most were stricken with gold fever and left San Francisco as soon as they could to head out to the mining camps. San Francisco needed builders, and James had learned carpentry back on Nantucket, having helped to rebuild the town after the fire.

In short order, James was hired by William H. Bovee to help build a spice and coffee mill. Bovee had owned a coffee mill in New York City that had burned down, prompting him to join the flood of men seeking their fortunes in California. Bovee's Pioneer Steam Coffee and Spice Mills was the first coffee mill in San Francisco. Business was lucrative as the miners thirsted for coffee and did not want to waste time roasting their own beans.

In 1851, James's brothers returned from the gold fields. Like most of the forty-niners, they had not struck it rich. Edward returned to Nantucket. Henry stayed in San Francisco and opened a whale oil business next door to Bovee's coffee mill.

James decided that it was his turn to seek his fortune in the gold fields. He took a load of spices and coffee to sell in the mining camps and sent orders for more back to Bovee. He had moderate luck as a miner, finding enough gold in Sonoma to open his own store in a camp called Yankee Jim's, where he stayed for two years. He then sold his store and moved back to San Francisco, where he was immediately reemployed by Bovee, this time as a clerk.

While James had been gone, Bovee had taken on a partner, Ira Marden, and they had built a new mill. In 1859, Bovee sold his share of the business to James, who was only twenty-four. The young man quickly became an important business leader in the growing city.

The Civil War disrupted the coffee business, and in 1865, Marden and Folger declared bankruptcy. Somehow, James bought out his partner and, after a decade of hard work, managed to pay off all the company's creditors. He changed the company's name to J.A. Folger and Company.

As San Francisco and California grew and prospered, so did his company. Folger's salesmen roamed the West hawking coffee and spices. Despite his success, James did not forget Nantucket, and he and his family visited the island for several summers. Unfortunately, James died suddenly of a massive heart attack in 1889, when he was just fifty-four. His son James Folger II, twenty-six, took over the company, incorporating it the year after his father's death with his two siblings, Ernest and Elizabeth. Under their leadership, the company continued to grow. Coffee became more refined, and Folgers offered a variety of blends, its most expensive called Folger's Golden Gate Coffee.

In 1905, the company moved into a new building on the waterfront incorporating the latest technology. When the massive San Francisco earthquake hit months later, Folgers was one of the few buildings that survived, thanks to pilings driven deep into the ground. In fact, the U.S. Marines used it as a base from which to battle the fires that raged after the earthquake using a gigantic hose and a fireboat. Despite the fact that the building itself escaped unscathed, the giant flywheel that operated the steam engine had suffered a crack, and the company could not roast beans. It moved its operation across the bay to Oakland, and the ground coffee was barged back across to the stricken city, desperate for coffee. In the early days of the disaster, San Franciscans were given Folgers coffee for free.

Within a month, the flywheel was replaced, and the company was back in business. Folgers expanded and opened a new plant in Kansas City in 1908.

Germany's naval blockade of the East Coast during World War I benefited San Francisco because much shipping shifted to the West. Fortuitously for the Folgers, San Francisco became one of the world's most important ports for coffee.

Like his father, James A. Folger II died in his early fifties. His elder son, James A. Folger III, was in college when his father died, so the leadership of the company went to his uncle Ernest in 1921. Ernest Folger streamlined the company by selling the spice and baking powder part of the business in order to concentrate on coffee. During the Roaring Twenties, Ernest took advantage of new advertising practices: billboards, magazine advertisements and radio advertisements and sponsorships. For example, the company sponsored a radio variety show called *Folgeria*, heard throughout the Midwest.

Against all odds, the company survived the Depression. As the economy crashed, there was a glut of coffee beans due to overplanting in South

America. There was such a surplus in Brazil that coffee beans were burned for heat and used to repair dirt roads. When Ernest Folger died in 1936, James A. Folger III became the president of the company. A third plant opened in Houston, Texas, and Folger's offices in El Salvador, Guatemala and Mexico ensured that Folgers had access to the choicest beans.

World War II created a huge demand for coffee. Soldiers demanded coffee at the front, and by then, office and factory workers had built-in coffee breaks. Despite the demand, the company struggled. Steel was scarce, workers were scarce and finding ships to transport coffee beans was difficult. Coffee rationing presented a further complication. Folgers substituted glass for its normal steel cans, but the result was less than satisfactory. The company appealed to the public to collect cans, but then they had to be properly cleaned. Another challenge was the variety of containers that resulted from the public appeal. It was not until 1948 that the glass jars were phased out and standardized steel cans were put back into production.

The next challenge was the advent of instant coffee. In 1953, Folgers produced its first jar of instant coffee, but it was a failure. Customers said it did not meet the standard they had come to expect of Folgers coffee, and the company took it out of production. It was not until 1958 that Folgers launched its version of instant coffee with a flurry of advertising. This time, the product was a success; business soared, and more plants were built.

In 1963, Folgers was bought by Procter and Gamble, and in 2008, it was acquired by the J.M. Smucker Company. According to *Business Week* in August 2013, Folgers Coffee is still the leading brand of coffee sold in the United States.

Meanwhile, coffee continued to make history back on Nantucket. In 1873, the *Minmaneuth* ran aground in the fog on the south shore near Miacomet Pond. En route to Boston from Rio de Janeiro, the *Minmaneuth* was carrying four thousand pounds of coffee. Nantucketers and summer visitors trekked out to view the stranded ship and to watch the offloading operation. Once one thousand pounds of coffee was removed, the sails were raised and the ship floated freely. The coffee was taken to Nantucket Harbor, picked up by a packet boat and taken to Boston with little harm done. However, the grounding could have been a tragedy, and not long afterward a lifesaving station was built at Surfside. The building, now Nantucket's Youth Hostel, owes part of its existence to the American demand for coffee.

It is not clear when Nantucket got its first true coffee shop. The first advertisement referring to a coffee shop was for the Liberty Coffee Shop in

Crowds looking out at the stranded *Minmaneuth* amid bags of offloaded coffee in July 1873. *Nantucket Historical Association.*

the summer of 1920. Located at 1 Liberty Street, it advertised "tea, coffee, cake, light breakfasts, cold lunches, ice cream and college ices."

Numerous coffee shops followed, catering to the summer trade. There was a coffee shop in the 1930s at the Hotel Overlook now called the Veranda House, and Charlotte's Coffee Shop served up coffee and pastries in 'Sconset in the 1940s. The Jolly Beaver Coffee House served coffee in town at 21 Centre Street. It wrongly boasted to be "Nantucket's Oldest Coffee House" but did not open until 1959. For about a decade in the early 1970s, there was the Sea Gull Coffee Shop in Madaket.

Another establishment associated with the word "coffee" was Cy's Green Coffee Pot, a popular year-round family restaurant that was a mainstay of Nantucket's dining scene for over forty-six years. Cy's was a full restaurant,

Cy's Green Coffee Pot on South Water Street, circa 1960s, now the site of NIXS Brewpub. *Nantucket Historical Association.*

not really a coffee shop, but coffee *was* served in green pots. Established in 1932 by Simon and Rose Kaufman, Cy's opened its doors on Middle Pearl Street, now known as India Street, but in 1936 moved to South Water Street where NIXS is now located. Regulars called Rose Kaufman "Ma." After Cy's death in 1965, his daughter Zelda and her husband, Milt Zlotin, operated the restaurant until their retirement in 1979, when they closed the doors.

Nantucket continues to be involved in coffee roasting, although not on the scale of Folgers. In 1993, Wes Van Cott opened Nantucket Coffee Roasters, capitalizing on the popularity of gourmet coffees. Although not born on the island, Wes spent time on Nantucket as a youngster when his father was a chef at the Gordon Folger, now the Nantucket Hotel. Wes spent the rest of his childhood in Tucson, but when his father returned to the island a decade later to run the bakery for Walter Beineke's commissary out of the Sweet Shoppe on Main Street (now the site of Met on Main), Wes returned to the island for a few years before moving once again.

However, after seven years in Maine, Wes moved back to Nantucket, where he worked as a sous chef at the India House and in the wallpaper and painting trade. Although he had little experience with coffee, he borrowed money in 1993 to buy a roaster. And as he says, "the rest is history."

Nantucket Coffee Roasters has grown steadily. It now roasts approximately seventy thousand pounds of coffee each year at its roaster on Teasdale Circle. Most of the business is local, with over fifty Nantucket establishments selling blends of its coffee. It also has an online presence and ships coffee around the world. Likewise, beans come to Nantucket from all over the world. Wes is well aware of Nantucket's Folger connection and enjoys pointing out that he lives on Folger Avenue.

Thirteen years ago, Nantucket Coffee Roasters opened The Bean, a popular year-round coffee shop. But there are many options for tourists and Nantucketers to grab a cub of coffee today. Besides The Bean, people gather for coffee at the pharmacy on Main Street, Handlebars on Washington Street and at The Green on West Creek Road. Cups are grabbed at The Hub, Cumberland Farms, Island Coffee, Espresso to Go and Fast Forward. Much of that coffee is roasted locally, supplied by Nantucket Coffee Roasters.

Opposite, top: Wes Van Cott, owner of Nantucket Coffee Roasters since 1993, in front of his coffee roasters. *Mark White.*

Opposite, bottom: Coffee beans from around the world waiting to be roasted at Nantucket Coffee Roasters. *Mark White.*

10

Critters on Nantucket, from Sheep to Prairie Dogs

The whale is the animal most associated with Nantucket's history. Nantucketers made their fame and fortune from whaling, and images of whales are ubiquitous. Whales festoon all manner of souvenirs from T-shirts to coffee mugs. The whale is the symbol of Nantucket High School. Whale skeletons hang in the hallway of the high school and at the Whaling

Docked fishing boats, 2014. *Mark White.*

Museum. Whales still inhabit the waters around the island, but their numbers are depleted, and most tourists never catch a glimpse of a real whale.

While whales no longer dominate Nantucket's wildlife, there are other animals that draw visitors to our shores. Through the foresight of environmental agencies, half of the island is protected from development, preserving habitat for a rich variety of wildlife.

Although there is no longer a commercial fishing fleet on the island, Nantucket does boast one of the best offshore sport fishing areas on the East Coast, and there are a number of charter boats for hire. Sea bass, bluefish, tuna, shark, fluke, marlin and bonito are among the fish that are caught. Every August since 2001, there has been the several-day "Big Game Battle" fishing tournament that raises money for a different charity every year. In 2013, the tournament raised over $30,000 for Nantucket's S.T.A.R. program that provides therapeutic and accessible recreation and adaptive sports to children with a range of disabilities and challenges. In 2014, the tournament raised money for the Boys and Girls Club of Dorchester.

Nantucket has the last remaining wild bay scallop commercial fishery in the United States. The familiar scallop shell is almost as associated with the island today as the whale. Commercial scalloping adds millions of dollars every year to the local economy. To keep commercial scalloping viable, Nantucket supports a scallop propagation program that releases millions of scallop larvae into the water every year. Commercial scallop season runs from November through March and is strictly regulated. In November 2012, storms threw seed scallops up on the beaches in the harbor, threatening the survival of Nantucket's bay scallops, which only live for two years. Islanders from all walks of life turned up by the dozens in the cold to rake up the young scallops and return them to the water.

Nantucket is a bird watcher's paradise with its grasslands, marshes, beaches, moors and protected habitat. People come from all over the world to witness the migrations that pass over the island. The Linda Loring Nature Foundation has sponsored a birding festival in October since 2000 that has quickly become a major birding event. In 2012, the first grey-tailed tattler seen in the eastern United States was spotted during the festival, and in 2013, a rare calliope hummingbird was spotted. During the winter of 2014, dozens of snowy owls irrupted on the island, bringing birders to Nantucket.

In the early days, islanders depended on farms and farm animals for dairy products, meat and clothing. The early settlers found the island ideal for sheep grazing with its accessible ponds and rolling hills. With no predators,

The view looking northeast over Steamboat Wharf and Easy Street, circa 1910, showing tracks and cars of the Nantucket Railroad and Brant Point in the distance. *Nantucket Historical Association.*

Herd of sheep in the winter, circa 1890. *Nantucket Historical Association.*

the sheep were allowed to roam freely. In fact, until eclipsed by whaling, raising sheep was a mainstay of Nantucket's economy. At its height, it is estimated that up to fifteen thousand sheep roamed on the undivided land known as the Sheep Commons. The town erected the Newtown Gate to attempt to keep sheep out of town, but it was not particularly effective; there

Sheep grazing along the Milestone Road, circa 1910. *Nantucket Historical Association.*

are many accounts of sheep making themselves a nuisance in the streets. In the 1770s, the town appointed shepherds to tend to the welfare of the sheep, especially during harsh weather.

Pens were eventually erected to enclose the sheep during winter, and hay was put out to prevent them from starving. According to shepherdess Jessica Pycosz, penning the sheep had unfortunate consequences because their enclosure led to overgrazing; the health of the sheep declined as the animals had less access to a variety of vegetation.

Every June from the mid-eighteenth century until the mid-nineteenth century, the sheep were rounded up, washed and sheared. The three-day event became the most important festival on the island; townspeople gathered to buy and sell items, picnic and, in later years, to dance. Marching bands sometimes came from off island parading from the wharf to the fairgrounds. By the early 1850s, raising sheep on a grand scale was a thing of the past, and the practice of free-roaming sheep declined as the common lands came under private ownership.

Cattle were also important to the early farms, although not as important to the town's economy as sheep. Most were dairy cows. The town farm in Quaise kept cows for milk and provided the inhabitants with work. An article in 1855 reported there were 558 "milch" or milk cows on the island. A letter to the editor a few years later complained that some farmers carelessly let their cows wander on the public streets. In 1917, many island cows had to be slaughtered when they were infected with tuberculosis.

Horses arrived on the island almost as early as the white settlers did and were the basis of early transportation. A visitor in 1825 remarked on

Off to a sheep shearing in a calash in 1895. *Nantucket Historical Association.*

"the curious" horse-drawn carts unique to Nantucket called "calashes." He thought the calashes were "awkward and inconvenient," requiring the driver to stand up "instead of sitting down" as was common off island. He also noted that they were almost noiseless because of the deep sand in the town's streets.

More commonly, horses were saddled and ridden. There were occasional arraignments for reckless riding and racing. For example, in 1834, three young men were charged and fined for "riding furiously" on Orange Street, "endangering the limbs and lives of the inhabitants." In 1852, the selectmen called a special town meeting to prevent the kicking of footballs in the street, partly because of the danger to "gentlemen driving spirited horses." In 1881, the selectmen voted to fine everyone one dollar who rode a horse on the town sidewalks. And once the island built bicycle paths, islanders complained that some riders damaged the new paths by the "thoughtless" driving of horses on them. "Keep horses where they belong," editorialized the *Inquirer and Mirror*.

Most horses were used on the island farms in a variety of well-known chores. A report in the mid-1850s noted that there were 346 horses on

Wagons on Orange Street, circa 1860. *Nantucket Historical Association.*

the island. In 1853, the newspaper reported that Edward C. Joy was the first island farmer to operate a mowing machine drawn by two horses and noted that other Nantucketers planned to order similar machines.

By the mid-1840s, it was acceptable for women to ride horseback. In 1843, the *Inquirer* noted that it was "glad to observe" that horseback riding had become "fashionable" among the "young ladies of this goodly island," praising riding as "healthful and invigorating." The editor wrote that it was pleasant "to see a fine woman mounted upon a spirited steed which she has under perfect management and control."

There are no public stables on the island today, although there are a number of privately owned horses.

Islanders today have a love affair with dogs. The *Inquirer and Mirror* has a blog dedicated to photos of island dogs, and there are many favorite dog-walking trails. Labrador Retrievers are ideal for the island with their love of the water and easy-going nature, and many are found on construction sites. More and more, islanders own "Mississippi Mutts," abandoned dogs brought from the South and rehabilitated by Nantucket Safe Harbor for Animals before being put up for adoption. In 2014, one lucky rescued dog flew out of Nantucket on Air Force Two, having been adopted by the son of Vice President Joe Biden. And being a wealthy community, there are many purebreds on the island, some having been shown at the Westminster Dog Show.

In the early days of Nantucket, however, dogs did not live the pampered lives of today's pets. Most dogs lived on farms and were used for herding sheep. Some became public nuisances. In 1830, the newspaper reported there were too many barking dogs in town and suggested that no one be allowed to keep more than one. There were, of course, some dogs kept as pets. In 1853, a little dog named Pink was lost; the owner offered a reward if he was found. As far back as the mid-1800s, dogs were supposed to wear collars. An article complained that too many uncollared dogs were running wild in the streets, and people threatened to shoot them. The selectmen voted to require all dogs to be licensed and to wear a collar with their owner's name. Yet in 1859, the newspaper reported that one-third of the island's dogs were still unlicensed and continued to run loose. Town police were ordered to destroy all the unlicensed dogs they found. Yet problems with unlicensed dogs persisted. In the 1870s, there were reports of fines levied on those who had failed to license their dogs. Not all the dogs fit the description of wild dogs running amuck. For example, the socially prominent Mrs. Benjamin Sharp was fined the hefty sum of $32.78 in 1878 for "keeping two unlicensed dogs." (Dr. Benjamin Sharp was the zoologist on Robert Perry's first trip to Greenland in 1891 and a founder of the Nantucket Cottage Hospital.)

No "wild" mammals are native to the island unless you include small rodents such as mice or voles. The island has no native cats, squirrels, chipmunks, possum, skunk or big game.

The island has a few varieties of harmless snakes, including common garter snakes and water snakes. There are several varieties of turtles, including large snapping turtles in Long Pond where children use chicken legs to raise them to the surface. There is one species of salamander; there are frogs, including noisy peepers, which are abundant.

The island has a large deer population with a density estimated at around forty to fifty per square mile. The Massachusetts Division of Fisheries and Wildlife recommends an optimum density of no more than fifteen deer per square mile. While many people regard the white-tailed deer as "cute," their association with tick-borne diseases is a cause of concern, especially as the deer have no natural enemies on the island aside from people. The growing herds are disruptive to native plant populations and pose problems to motorists.

Deer in Nobadeer Valley. *Mark White.*

Local legend claims that the first deer were deliberately brought to the island in the early 1920s; however, the Nantucket Conservation Foundation disputes that. Archaeological evidence shows that deer have been here since Nantucket became an island. However, the early deer were overhunted and became extinct. So, what is true is that deer were reintroduced to the island in 1922 when an exhausted deer was rescued by the fishing sloop *Antonia*. Game warden William H. Jones was notified, and the buck was taken to the woods off the 'Sconset Road. A summer resident, Breckinridge Long, sent two does to Squam Swamp to keep the buck company. They became fruitful and multiplied.

The first deer hunt in modern times was in early 1935, despite an initial outcry from the board of selectmen. The herd was estimated at the time as approximately four hundred. The first hunt yielded about thirty-five deer killed. Even then, locals worried that the island could not support the number of deer due to lack of food and complained about the damage that the starving deer were wreaking on local gardens. The second deer hunt took place in December the same year, this time with the support of the selectmen. Unfortunately, one hunter was killed and another injured, and the selectmen telegraphed Governor James Curley to end the season early, which he did. George Sylvia, a Nantucket resident who had been acting as a hunting guide to a group of off-islanders when he was shot, left a wife and four children. For several weeks it was not clear who had shot Sylvia, but at a hearing, Winfield Cornett of Boston tearfully confessed that he had accidentally shot the guide. No charges were levied, and the shooting was declared an accident. The injured hunter, William Madeiros, was shot in the face and shoulders by a man hunting the same deer from another direction.

In 2013, over eight hundred deer were hunted and killed on the island, and there are those who believe that the hunting season should be extended in order to eliminate more deer, including Dr. Timothy Lepore, who cites the growth of tick-borne diseases.

Other animals were reported on the island, most of which have disappeared. Some were introduced on purpose, and others probably hitched rides on board ships. Most were unwanted "varmints." Rats have been long associated with ships, and Nantucket's rats are no exception. Just before Christmas in 1898, the paper complained that rats were multiplying "all over the island." And many an older islander remembers shooting rats at the dump before it became the present landfill.

An article in the *Inquirer and Mirror* on October 21, 1886, reported "righteous indignation" because five foxes had been surreptitiously "set loose" near Gibbs Pond. The probable motive was to start foxhunting on the island. Fingers were pointed at Edwin J. Hulbert and Harold Williams. Hulbert wrote a letter to the paper denying any involvement with foxes by him or Williams and he offered a twenty-five-dollar reward to anyone who caught a fox and ten dollars for information about who released the animals. The newspaper warned that the foxes needed to be exterminated before the "sly marauders" got out of control. The following year, Sidney B. Folger shot a fox that was put on display for several days at the 'Sconset market of D.W. Burgess and Sons. The paper reported that his was one of "numerous" foxes shot that winter. The foxhunts were successful, and no fox was sighted until 1907, when another fox was allegedly spotted but never spotted again. In 1947, an article in the *Boston Globe* bemoaned the lack of foxes on the island for the sport of foxhunting, writing that would-be foxhunters on Nantucket had to use rabbits for practice. However, no other foxes were ever secretly released, and the notion of foxhunting disappeared.

Other animals were deliberately introduced for hunters, including quail, pheasant and grouse. Quail were released at various times on the island, including in the 1890s and the 1930s. Eight cages of grouse were released in 1893, but none survived the first winter. The Nantucket Sportsmen's Club released pheasants in 1936, and there are still occasional pheasants spotted on the island. There were also pigeon shoots, although it is unlikely that the pigeons were imported.

In 1858, it was reported that there was an "abundant" number of raccoons in Trott's Swamp, which is now a part of the Nantucket Conservation Foundation's Sanford Farm property. A hunt was organized that September that evidently took care of the problem, although a single raccoon was killed in 1893, stuffed and put on display in a pharmacy on Main Street.

In the 1890s, prairie dogs were introduced to Nantucket, although it is not clear who brought them or why. They quickly proliferated and became a nuisance, mostly in the area of Nobadeer. For one, their holes were dangerous to horses, which could easily break a leg falling into one. In 1900, the town embarked on a mission to eradicate the prairie dogs and asked the public to report areas where they were living. The town signed a $500 contract with N.D. Nutt, an off-island exterminator, to get rid of the pests, and by April, it was reported that "the large colonies of prairie dogs" at Nobadeer were "practically extinct." None have been seen since.

Rabbits have multiplied on the island with few enemies other than birds of prey and automobiles. Several varieties of rabbits live on the island, but by far the most numerous are eastern cottontails, rabbits not native to New England. They were purposely brought to Nantucket for hunting in the 1880s and provide an example of a nonnative species pushing out a native one. There are only a few spots on the island where the original New England cottontails still exist. In November 2013, the Nantucket Conservation Foundation reported finding a rabbit that was positively identified as a New England cottontail, the first positive sighting in decades. Nantucket may also host a few black-tailed jackrabbits, another species not seen recently but which is thought to still exist. There have been a few recent sightings of snowshoe hares, another species introduced to the island for hunting but that are now rarely seen.

Like the white-tailed deer, rabbits are hosts to ticks and are so numerous that it would be exceedingly difficult to significantly reduce their population.

There has been a recent effort to reintroduce sheep to the island's landscape. The Nantucket Conservation Foundation began a research project in 2005 to see how sheep would impact native flowers and grasses and to ascertain whether sheep could be useful in stopping the encroachment of woody vegetation and poison ivy. It is believed that sheep might help to restore some of the original sand plain habitat of the island described by Henry David Thoreau in 1854, when he wrote that there was not a tree to be seen, except those deliberately planted in gardens. Jessica Pycosz managed the Squam Farm flock of approximately one hundred sheep for the Nantucket Conservation Foundation for over six years. She reported on the success of the experiment, noting that island-born are more willing to eat Nantucket's plants than those imported here. It took some trial and error to find a breed suitable for the island. The sheep are a mix of hardy sheep that can jump through the island's tangled underbrush. Movable pens enable the sheep to be moved from area to area, depending on the time of year and the nutritious plants that are available. Pycosz reported that the sheep have been successful at eating some invasive species without harming native vegetation. The farm shears the sheep, reminiscent of the yearly sheep shearing festival, and the wool is sold locally.

II

A Lamentation

If you drove the Polpis Road in the 1960s, you are likely to remember the special beauty of Folger's Marsh at that time. The marsh is still beautiful, still serene, still with the look of an inlet as its blue waters spread to the right of the Nantucket Shipwreck and Life Saving Museum. It is still tempting to slow down as one drops down the hills on either side of the marsh and pass by what continues to be one of the treasures of the island. Painters still set up their easels, and tour buses slow as they

Folger's Marsh. *Mark White.*

Two swans with the look of those now absent from Folger's Marsh. *Mark White.*

pass by. But not for the reasons they once did. Once there were swans in Folger's Marsh.

On January 1, 1960, the *Inquirer and Mirror* published a photograph of two swans, with the following caption: "These 'wild' swans were photographed at the salt marsh near the Gordon Farm on the Polpis Road. The graceful birds attracted much attention but were not wild. They belong to Stephen Peabody." This seems to be the first public indication of mute swans on Nantucket. The mute swan is a species not native to the United States, as tundra swans are, but a variety brought to this continent from Eurasia in the late nineteenth century to enhance the private estates and gardens of the wealthy around New York. In time, some swans escaped and spread up the East Coast. In this case, a pair came to Folger's Marsh, which lies just below Harry Gordon hill, brought by Stephen Peabody. All the many mute swans now on the island may derive from this initial pair.

A year and a half after their first mention, the July 27, 1962 *Inquirer and Mirror* again published a photograph of the swans in the marsh: "This beautiful family of swans are the center of attraction for motorists traveling the Polpis Road. Papa Swan is nearest to the camera and he is constantly on guard against the possibility of intruders while Mama Swan is guiding the four cygnets to the best feeding places."

Swans are monogamous. Where space is limited, a pair may live alone with their offspring, the "ugly ducklings" of the Hans Christian Anderson story. Such a family nested at Folger's Marsh. For a considerable time, a single pair occupied this beautiful setting. The solitude of the birds and their stunning beauty in that peaceful scene appealed to all who saw them. Well, not to everyone. For the last forty years, no swans have lived in Folger's Marsh. For those who drove by them, day after day, year after year in the 1960s and took pleasure in them, Folger's Marsh seems today a crime scene, a place of grief.

In the 1960s, mute swans in Nantucket were an unusual sight and not thought by most a danger to vegetation or other birds on the island. In those days, Hummock and Long Ponds did not swarm with swans as they do today. They were not considered nuisances. Today, many environmentalists think their numbers need controlling and not the protection once enjoyed under the 1916 Migratory Bird Treaty. In 2005, the United States Department of the Interior declared mute swans a nonnative invasive species and stripped them of federal protection. Now, in many places, they can be killed on sight. But not in Massachusetts. In Massachusetts they are still (for the time being) protected.

In the 1960s, when new to the island, mute swans were a pleasure to see and enjoy and for most on the island not a problem. Nonetheless, they were endangered.

For example, on May 19, 1966, the *Inquirer and Mirror* headlined a story "Swan-Killing May Be Latest Island 'Sport.'" A large white swan, "believed to be one of the original pair brought to the Island several years ago by the late Steven Peabody of Polpis, has been found dead floating in the harbor waters near the Island Marine Service bulkhead off Washington Street." Police Chief Wendell Holmes said spots of red paint on the body indicated it might have been struck, killed and perhaps "run down deliberately by a fast boat." Again, the paper identifies swans with Polpis: "The swans have been frequenting the harbor area through the winter and many people have gone to the Children's Beach to toss them bread and other food. They spend their summers in an inlet off the Polpis Road where the people are able to park their cars and watch them dive for food." These, it is suggested, "have propagated," leading to there being "numerous cygnets in various parts of the inner harbor," with some having been seen even in Long Pond.

Six months later, the December 1, 1966 *Inquirer and Mirror* reported "Three Swans Shot." The article described the killing as "a particularly irresponsible act" and as "another set back" to "the wild life assets of the Island." These swans, readers are told, have made their home for some time in Long Pond. Interestingly, the article assumes the only explanation for such a wanton killing would be "one or more misguided hunters" thinking the swans were eating the pond food also used by ducks, exactly one of the problems with large numbers of them being in that pond today. The article declared, "Such an idea is of course not realistic as there is plenty of food for both."

The final *Inquirer and Mirror* article on swans in Folger's Marsh is a front-page photo on January 9, 1969. Again, the paper emphasizes how attractive they were to passing motorists: "Four swans are wintering at Folger's Creek in Polpis and attract a lot of attention from passing motorists who stop along the Polpis Road as the swans paddle around in the icy water seeking food."

There is something about swans—something about their elegance, their grace, their size, their long arched necks that seem to arise directly from the water, their pairing for life, their protectiveness of their young and their family groups—that appeals to the human heart. From classical times, the phrase "swan song" has referred to their love and loyalty, the pain at a loved partner's death supposedly leading "mute" swans into beautiful song. Positive references to swans as like human beings in their fidelity are common in religions and cultures around the world. In myth, Helen of Troy is born of Zeus, who, disguised as a swan, impregnates Leda, the Queen of Sparta. She gives birth to Helen, whose beauty is more perfect than the gods themselves, and leads to all the troubles in Troy recounted by Homer.

William Butler Yeats tells the story of Leda's rape in his poem "Leda and the Swan." On a quieter note, there is also his poem "The Wild Swans at Coole," which in its closing lines portrays something of the pull and appeal of the Polpis swans:

> *Unwearied still, lover by lover,*
> *They paddle in the cold*
> *Companionable streams or climb the air;*
> *Their hearts have not grown old;*
> *Passion or conquest, wander where they will,*
> *Attend upon them still.*
>
> *But now they drift on the still water,*
> *Mysterious, beautiful;*
> *Among what rushes will they build,*
> *By what lake's edge or pool*
> *Delight men's eyes when I awake some day*
> *To find they have flown away?*

Flown away? Or killed? What happened to the wild (or tame) swans of Folger's Marsh? After 1969, they are never again mentioned in the press. From that time until now, their presence has been in their absence. There are no swans in Folger's Marsh. Did they fly away to more attractive areas to nest and feed, perhaps in Quaise? Or were they murdered?

For many who remember the Folger's Marsh swans in the 1960s, it is a story of murder. But if so, a murder not recorded in the island's paper of record. Some remember the swans as having been found dead in the marsh, a father and mother swan and three or four or five cygnets. In the rushes at the edge of the marsh, police, it was said, found an area where grass was pressed down as if someone had lain in wait. Spent shotgun shells were supposedly scattered about—all indicating a planned, premeditated ambush.

But there may be another explanation. In an August 3, 1978 letter to the *Inquirer and Mirror*, Peg Kelley of Quaise tells of swans that have nested "in the creeks at the University of Massachusetts Field Station." One of these swans presented himself in front of her house every day at about 4:00 p.m. "He made a funny little noise halfway between a purr and a cackle!" Although apprehensive at first, Ms. Kelley began to feed the swan, leading to a "delightful association." She called him "Big Bird" after the Sesame Street character. She fed him, and like clockwork at 4:00 p.m., he would come looking for her and the bread she would give him. Once when he didn't arrive at his usual time she assumed he had stayed with "his lady love" while she gave birth to her cygnets. And when they were indeed born, was Big Bird ever "proud, and protective!" The four "fuzzy greyish baby swans… floated around the creeks for several days, and sunned themselves on the bank—and then one day they were not there." A friend thought they might be at the marina where other swans gathered. "I didn't know the truth," writes Ms. Kelley, "until I read the first letter in the paper about their having been shot." "To me," she wrote, "it was the loss of a good friend." She added fifty dollars to what Jane Carlee had offered "for information leading to the apprehension of the murderer of Big Bird and his family."

One week later, a front-page article in the August 10, 1978 *Inquirer and Mirror* by W.N. Tiffney of the UMass Field Station set minds at rest, at least about "Big Bird," alias "Charlie." Charlie had been found alive and well in Shawkemo with his spouse, "Leda," and four cygnets. "Mrs. Edith F. Andrews, Nantucket's respected ornithologist, made positive identification of 'Charlie' through his pinioned right wing." Charlie, we are told, was one of the four original mute swans brought to the island by the late Stephen Peabody and the only one of the four to breed successfully. Stephen Peabody

Today's multitude of swans, Hummock Pond. *Mark White.*

had pinioned (removed the primary feathers from) Charlie's right wing, making him unable to fly. Therefore, it was asserted, Charlie "(though still an off-islander) is a year 'round resident and not simply a migrant summer visitor." He and Leda, thought to be the fourth Mrs. Charlie, had desired a change of scene in exchanging Quaise for Shawkemo. In this case, clearly there was no murder.

Perhaps something similar happened at Folger's Marsh in the 1960s. Perhaps not. But for many who were around at that long-ago time and still drive the Polpis Road, either toward town or to Wauwinet or Quidnet, the absence of the Folger's Marsh swans is felt as a sharp pain, an absence visible, a question.

In all these years, why have swans not returned to the marsh? Do they avoid it because they know something most of us do not know or have forgotten?

Bibliography

Arno, Lucia. "Silk Industry Lived Briefly for Nantucketers in 1800s." *Cape Cod Times*, December 26, 1977.

Banner, Earl. "Rabbits Wish There Were Foxes on Nantucket." *Boston Globe*, August 24, 1947.

Chase, Sidney. "The Story of Golf," Nantucket Historical Association, 1921.

Dudley, Myron S. "Silk Industry in Nantucket." *Historic Nantucket* (October 1963).

Gamble, J.C. "A History of Nantucket's Golf Courses." *Historic Nantucket* (October 1998).

Grieder, James. "Unearthing the Dead: The Search for Nantucket's Forgotten Heroes." http://tuckernuckjim.tripod.com/hidden/id16.html.

Inquirer. 1821–1865.

Inquirer and Mirror. 1821–2014.

Islander. March 10, 1840–March 18, 1843.

Jones, George W. "A Brief Account of Whaleship Building on Nantucket." *Historic Nantucket* (January 1966).

———. "Nantucket's Busy Days of 150 Years Ago." *Historic Nantucket* (October 1981).

Karberg, Jen. "Thinking About Deer Browse 'Cause It's Hunting Season." Blog, November 28, 2012.

Karttunen, Frances Ruley. *The Other Islanders: People Who Pulled Nantucket's Oars.* New Bedford, MA: Spinner Publications, 2005.

Mann, Albert W. *History of the Forty-fifth Regiment: Massachusetts Volunteer Militia.* Boston: Wallace Spooner, 1908.

Manville, Michael. "A Hall of Amusement, and No Other Purpose." *Historic Nantucket* (May 1999).

Massachusetts Acts of 1845. Chapters 14 and 214. Massachusetts State Archives.

Massachusetts Adjutant-General's Office. *Massachusetts Soldiers, Sailors, and Marines in the Civil War—1861–1865*. 8 vols. Norwood, MA: Norwood Press, 1932.

Massachusetts House of Representatives. *Journal of the House of Representatives, 1845*. Massachusetts State Archives.

Massachusetts Senate. *Journal of the Senate, 1845*. Massachusetts State Archives.

Massachusetts State House Vaults. Seven petitions presented to the House, 1845.

Massachusetts Vital Records, Nantucket, 1662–1900.

Military Records. Ancestry.com.

Miller, Richard F. *Harvard's Civil War: A History of the Twentieth Massachusetts Volunteer Infantry*. Lebanon, NH: University Press of New England, 2005.

Miller, Richard F., and Robert F. Mooney. *The Civil War: The Nantucket Experience, Including the Memoirs of Josiah Fitch Murphey*. Nantucket, MA: Wesco Publishing, 1994.

Monaghan, James. "Anti-Slavery on Nantucket." *Proceedings of the Nantucket Historical Association*. 1938, 23.

Mooney, Robert F. "The Nantucket Coffee Connection." *Nantucket Magazine* (Early Summer 1997).

Morral, Tobit. *A Backus Family History: A Nantucket Family Reflected in Newsprint, 1823–1976*. N.p., 2014.

Nantucket Atheneum. *The Bill of Fare*, June 21, 1842.

Nantucket Town Records. 1807–1900.

Nantucket Weekly Mirror. 1845–1865.

Penrose, Clement A. "Nantucket's First Swimming Pool Built on 'Sconset Beach." *Historic Nantucket* (April 1974).

Pension Records. Fold3.com.

Pommett, Terry. "Raising the Cup." *Historic Nantucket* (October 1995).

Sheppard, Steve. "The Best Links This Side of Scotland." *Historic Nantucket* (October 1996).

———. "On a Tour of the Island's Golf Courses, in Search of Nantucket's Best Holes." *Historic Nantucket* (December 2004).

Stackpole, Edouard. "Once Along the Waterfront." *Historic Nantucket* (April 1965).

Stanton, John. "A Gift from the Sea." *Nantucket Today* (August 2008).

Tamlyn, Anne Marie. "The Temperance Movement in Nantucket, 1820–1870." Research paper, 1975.

Town of Nantucket. Births, Deaths, Marriages: 1843–1849, 1861–1865.

Tyler, Betsy. "How the Deer (and Fox, and Prairie Dog, Among Others) Came to Nantucket." *Nantucket Magazine* (Winter 2004).

Van Cott, Wes. Interviewed by Barbara A. White, November 25, 2013.

White, Barbara Ann. *A Line in the Sand: The Battle to Integrate Nantucket's Public Schools, 1825–1847*. New Bedford, MA: Spinner Publications, 2009.

———. *Live to the Truth: The Life and Times of Cyrus Peirce, Crusader for American Public Education, Founder of the First Public Teacher Training School in the Nation.* N.p., 2014.

Young, Roger. "Bicycles and Nantucket." *Historic Nantucket* (Spring 1992).

Nantucket Historical Association Research Library

Applications for membership in Thomas M. Gardner, Post 207, Grand Army of the Republic, Collection 93, Folder 3.

Backus, Eddie. Oral History. N.d.

Barney Genealogical Record.

Blacks on Nantucket, Collection 222, Folder 9.

Edouard Stackpole Collection, Collection 335, Folder 293.

Folger Family Papers, Collection 118, Folder 25.

George Murphy Papers, Collection 497, Box 1.

Jetties Beach Pavilion and Bath House, Preservation Institute Reports, 2007.

Maps and Charts, Collection 1000, Drawer 6, Folder 3, No. 1 and No. 8.

Nantucket Improvement Society Records, 1890–1911, Collection 48.

Newhall, Ruth Waldo. *The Folger Way: Coffee Pioneering Since 1850*. Blue File. N.d.

The Pledge. June 18, 1844. Collection 78.

Records of Temperance Societies of Nantucket, 1834–1900, Collection 78.

Robert F. Mooney Research Files, Collection 447, Box 3.

Ships' Papers, Collection 15, Folder 177.

Zlotin, Zelda. *Once More at Cy's*. N.d.

About the Authors

F rank Morral has a PhD in English literature from Columbia University and an MA in counseling psychology from the College of St. Thomas in Minnesota. He taught in the English Department at Carleton College for forty-two years. His wife, Linda Backus Morral, was born on Nantucket in a family that had lived on the island for many generations. After visiting the island for longer and shorter periods each summer since 1964, they became full-time residents in 2006. Frank's interest in Nantucket history was quickened with the discovery at the Nantucket Historical Association of a GAR application written by his wife's great-grandfather George Allen Backus. A private in Company I, Twentieth Massachusetts Volunteer Infantry, he fought in all its battles from Antietam to Cold Harbor, where he was seriously wounded. Neither Linda nor her siblings knew anything of this history. The discovery of this hidden history in her family led to his current research on the military experiences of Nantucket's Civil War soldiers and sailors. Frank and his son Tobit Morral recently wrote and published a children's book, *The Shy Butterfly on Nantucket*, illustrated by Ellie Gottwald.

B arbara Ann White is a research fellow at the Nantucket Historical Association and a retired public school history teacher. She received her undergraduate degree from Marietta College and has an MA from Boston University and the University of Lancaster in England. She received a Rockefeller Grant to assist in her research while she was a graduate student in African American history at Boston University. The university published

her work on Nantucket's important role in early civil rights legislation in 1978. Her book *A Line in the Sand: The Battle to Integrate Nantucket Public Schools, 1825–1847*, published in 2006, is an expanded version of that work. She is also the author of *Live to the Truth: The Life and Times of Cyrus Peirce: Crusader for American Public Education, Founder of the First Public Teacher Training School in the Nation*, published in 2014. Her next book will be about Anna Gardner, the teacher at the African School who went south during the Civil War to teach freedmen. She lives on Nantucket with her husband, Mark, who is her research partner.